THIN RED LINE

Volume 2

**Tracing God's
Amazing Story
of Redemption
Through Scripture**

"THIN RED LINE" SERIES

Thin Red Line, Volume 1
Thin Red Line, Volume 2
Thin Red Line, Volume 3
Thin Red Line, Volume 4

VIDEOS

More New Hope Books by Kimberly Sowell

*Lost on a Familiar Road: Allowing God's Love to
Free Your Mind for the Journey*

Lost on a Familiar Road: eDevotional

Soul Shaping: Creating Compassionate Children

Journey to Confidence: Becoming Women of Influential Faith

Journey to Significance: Becoming Women of Divine Destiny

*Major Truths from the Minor Prophets: Power, Freedom, and Hope for
Women*, coauthors Edna Ellison and Tricia Scribner

A Passion for Purpose: 365 Daily Devotions for Missional Living

Women of the Covenant: Spiritual Wisdom from Women of the Bible

A Month of Miracles: 30 Stories of the Unmistakable Presence of God,
coauthors Edna Ellison, Joy Brown, Tricia Scribner,
Marie Alston, and Cherie Nettles

THIN RED LINE

Volume 2

Tracing God's Amazing Story of Redemption Through Scripture

KIMBERLY
SOWELL

NEW HOPE
PUBLISHERS
Gospel-Centered. Missions-Driven.

BIRMINGHAM, ALABAMA

New Hope® Publishers
PO Box 12065
Birmingham, AL 35202-2065
NewHopeDigital.com
New Hope Publishers is a division of WMU®.

Library of Congress Product Control Number: 2014955637

All Scripture quotations, unless otherwise indicated, are taken from the
New American Standard Bible®, Copyright © 1960, 1962, 1963, 1968,
1971, 1972, 1973, 1975, 1977, 1995 by The Lockman Foundation. Used by
permission.

Scripture quotations marked (NKJV) are taken from the New King James
Version. Copyright © 1982 by Thomas Nelson, Inc. Used by permission. All
rights reserved.

New Hope Publishers series Project Team: Tina Atchenson, Mark Bethea,
Jourdan Berry, Joyce Dinkins, Lynn Groom, Melissa Hall, Joshua Hays, Vicki
Huffman, Maegan Roper, and Kathryne Solomon.

Series cover design: Bruce Watford
Series interior design: Glynese Northam

ISBN: 978-1-59669-425-5
N154104 • 0215 • 2M1

DEDICATION

I wish to dedicate the "Thin Red Line" series to my wonderful church family, Second Baptist Church in Lancaster, South Carolina. Thank you for stepping out in faith as a church to experience God's *thin red line* of redemption together for a year of study. I love you all, and I appreciate your firm stand on the Word of God, your fervent love for Jesus Christ, and your heart that beats for missions. May God continue to bless Second Baptist Church as we move forward to bring glory to His name.

And for each church, Bible study group, and individual who will read this volume and journey along the *Thin Red Line*, may God enrich your walk with Christ and positively flood your heart and mind with His glorious redeeming love.

ACKNOWLEDGMENTS

Every book has its own birth story. The "Thin Red Line" series was born out of my home church's desire to understand fully how all the pieces of the Bible come together to paint one breathtaking picture of redemption. I can tell you that through my personal experience of journeying this *thin red line*, my walk with Christ has been taken to a new level because of my strengthened understanding of what God did to save my soul, and I adore Him all the more. I am excited about what God is going to do in your life and in your church because of this journey you are about to take through redemption's story.

I've tried to go back to the very beginning and retrace the steps of how this book series came into being. I can't remember if it first happened in my office, or my pastor's office; perhaps it was in the executive pastor's office . . . But I remember discussions about the life-changing power of the Word of God. I recall that our hearts were beating rapidly and our voices were escalating with excitement as we began to dream about what could happen if each person in our church began studying together, digging for ourselves to catch the "big picture" of Scripture. We started envisioning the spiritual growth and Bible literacy that God would bring to our people if we started in Genesis and marched through Scripture to thread together the evidence of God's plan from the very beginning—that God would send a Savior to save sin-wrecked humanity.

This church-wide emphasis coupled with the writing process required many people working together for a common purpose to make the "Thin Red Line" series a reality. Our church body embraced this 52-week journey as we studied together. Our weekly Bible study groups studied one lesson per week. Our pastor delivered sermons to reinforce and more fully develop where we were in the timeline as we studied redemption's history together. This was no isolated program; this was the theme of our church for an entire year, and we were blown away with how God transformed us through the power of His Word.

So many people are deserving of thanks:

Dr. Brian Saxon, pastor: Thank you, Pastor Brian, for being willing to take a risk and do something so "out of the box" for the sake of our church family's spiritual growth. Your desire for each person to know and understand God's plan of redemption ushered us to a deeper appreciation for God's great love for all of us.

Marshall Fagg, executive pastor: Preacher Marshall, thank you for helping to shape the vision and develop a format that made this study effective for everyone. Your doctrinal oversight and words of encouragement each week blessed me every step of the way. Whenever you teach God's Word, I am challenged by how deeply you love Jesus Christ.

Denise Johnston, LifeGroup director: Thank you, Denise, for providing leadership to our LifeGroup leaders and paving the way for an out-of-the-ordinary, yet extraordinary year of study. I appreciate your patience and the hard work you put into this process.

Kristie Taylor, editor: Kristie, I knew I could always count on your keen eye and wordsmithing abilities each week. Thank you not only for the editorial input but also the spiritual feedback to sharpen each lesson and encourage me as a writer.

Melanie Sanders, Pat Nobles, and Beth Center, administrative assistants: Thank you for your important role in getting the materials into the hands of our people each week, and always leading with a servant's heart. I appreciate your spirit of cooperation and kindness!

Small-Group Bible Study Leaders: To every leader who accepted the challenge to undergo a shift in how our church experienced small-group Bible studies, thank you for your willingness to stretch, grow, and embrace change. I thank God for the love and leadership that you provide each week as you connect with your small group with the heart of an undershepherd.

The Second Baptist Church Family: Writing this series was my distinct honor because I knew God was allowing me to connect with your lives at a very personal level: your love relationship with Jesus Christ. Thank you for your words of encouragement, your weekly study of God's Word, your celebration of biblical discoveries, and your willingness to live life together with everyone in our church family. I love you very much.

And as always, I want to extend a special thank you to New Hope Publishers team: for your firm commitment to provide Bible study materials that allow the Holy Spirit to be the teacher of each man and woman who opens the Scripture with a willing heart. I love your clarity of vision, and I am honored to partner with you.

CONTENTS

Conquered and Waiting

INTRODUCTION

Follow the Signs that Lead to the Cross

What are the Bible stories you remember from childhood? We all have our favorites. Noah's ark. Moses and the bulrushes, Moses and the burning bush, and Moses parting the Red Sea. David and Goliath. Abraham and Isaac. But which story comes first? What is the chronological order? And who was it that fought the battle of Jericho? Where do the judges fit into the Old Testament? When did the prophets come into the picture, and how do they fit into the rest of the Old Testament? When did Israel become a nation, and why is that even important? And can anyone give a clear explanation of how the Old Testament is linked to the New Testament?

If you are one of the blessed individuals who has had exposure to the Bible for much of your life, you could probably sit down with a blank sheet of paper and write down a long list of Bible stories you've studied in your lifetime. You may even be able to jot down a moral or biblical truth to correlate with each story. But so often our Bible study approach can be piecemeal and disjointed, jumping from one text to the next, that we find ourselves possessing an enormous pile of exquisite threads, appreciating each one for its individual beauty, yet unable to weave them together to see the intricate tapestry that is God's big picture.

The "Thin Red Line" series is an opportunity to start at the beginning in the Garden of Eden and walk chronologically through the Bible, tracing the link of commonality found in every book of the Bible: redemption. From beginning to end, God's Word points us to the Cross. The evidence is striking. The benefits reaped from the "Thin Red Line" series are many:

You'll be overwhelmed by God's intentionality. Looking at Scripture passages with one particular focus, God's plan of redemption, will show how He has painstakingly dropped evidence like breadcrumbs through time, leading to the Cross. In fact, throughout this study you'll find that sometimes God left breadcrumbs, but more often He provided large arrows with neon lights pointing people to the promised Savior, His Son, Jesus Christ.

You'll be overwhelmed by God's love. As you study God's master plan and the many ways God interacted with people to usher in their salvation, you cannot help but understand more deeply that humanity is completely undeserving of God's grace. From the beginning God has been consistent, and He has been faithful; you'll see in this study that from the beginning humans are consistently inconsistent and tend toward unfaithfulness. Why did God follow through with the plan? Why did God keep His promise by sending His own Son into this fallen world? It must be love.

You'll grow in Bible literacy. For those who traverse all 52 weeks, you will find a deeper understanding of how the different books of the Bible fit together and how the stories flow chronologically. I confess to you that as the writer, my Bible knowledge grew leaps and bounds as I sat down to march purposefully through time in studying redemption. The growth I experienced has made me a more passionate teacher of God's Word. Whether I'm teaching my children at home around the kitchen table or sharing God's Word in a more formal setting, I long for God's people to possess a working knowledge of the Bible. The "Thin Red Line" series provides a framework for understanding the overall history of Scripture.

You'll fall in love with the Old Testament. It's just a theory, but I believe that many Christians shy away from reading the Old Testament because they don't know the history, they can't figure out the relevance of some of the stories, and they don't see how its contents can deepen their walk with Christ. Prepare to be amazed! You'll fall in love with the Old Testament when you begin to hear its pages whispering the name of Jesus.

You'll fall in love with the New Testament. Follow the "Thin Red Line" series from beginning to end. Your heart is going to sing "glory hallelujah!" when you arrive at the manger, having gained a deeper appreciation for the Babe wrapped in swaddling clothes. When looking through redemption's lens, you'll understand the life of Jesus and the profound nature of every word He said and every act He performed. And how do the Book of Acts and the letters to the churches connect to redemption? Embrace the teachings of *Volume Four* of this series, and experience being a part of God's plan of redemption for all of the peoples of the world.

You'll go to new levels of friendship with your Bible study group. The format of the "Thin Red Line" series lends itself to meaningful, on-topic, highly relevant discussions for your study time together. Each lesson is designed to allow participants to walk away with a solid understanding of the Bible passage (you will remember the details of the story for days to come) and also specific applications from God's Word to put into practice in everyday life. The approach is both discussion-based and Bible-centered.

I pray that God will use this study series to enrich your relationship with Jesus and deepen your love for God's Word. May God's people never cease to be amazed at the grace of God, the Author of our redemption through Jesus Christ!

Kimberly

WELCOME TO THE
THIN RED LINE

Welcome to the *Thin Red Line*. Throughout Scripture, we see a beautiful scarlet thread of God's redemptive plan for humanity. From the beginning, He has implemented a divine strategy to save us from our sins and adopt us as His children. In this study, we will experience powerful life transformation as we understand and embrace how God has revealed Himself and His beautiful redemptive plan from cover to cover in His Holy Word.

Each lesson's small-group leader guide contains some specific components:

RED LINE DETAILS

- **Red Line Verse:** the memory verse for the lesson

- **Red Line Statement:** a statement of how the lesson relates to God's redemptive plan for mankind to be saved

- **Red Line Connection:** the theme of the lesson

- **Focal Passages:** the passages covered in the lesson

Hear—Listen Attentively to the Lesson
This section is the telling of the Bible story and its details from Scripture.

Search—Investigate the Facts of the Lesson

This section examines what is happening in the story, allowing each person to thoroughly digest what is being conveyed in the text. *You'll find group-leader discussion statements in italics.*

See—Find the Purpose of the Lesson

This section allows your small group to begin processing what God is teaching about Himself and how they can live for Him. Your group will discuss the significance of God's truths and how they apply to their lives. *You'll find group-leader discussion statements in italics.*

Live—Experience the Truth of the Lesson

This section is a crucial component of the lesson—sharing how God's Word is reshaping your hearts and minds to be strong disciples of Jesus Christ. In this section that closes each lesson, you will have the opportunity as the small-group leader to challenge your group to respond specifically and to implement this lesson in their lives the following week. *See discussion statements in italics.*

CONSISTENT INCONSISTENCY

How could we even begin to describe the nation of Israel in the days following the leadership of Moses? In this period of their history, their only consistency was their inconsistency. Some days they followed the Lord with passion and loyalty; other days they fell away from the Lord, living with total disregard for their God. They had godly leaders, followed by wicked leaders. Their level of obedience landed on both ends of the spectrum, while at other times they were at neither extreme but rather lukewarm and somewhere in between. However, God remained faithful to reveal Himself to His people, continuing to mark out for humanity a *thin red line* of redemption.

We shake our heads and wonder how God's chosen people could be so careless with the covenant relationship they enjoyed with God! But then we look in the mirror and realize that their story is perhaps not so different from our own. If ever there has been one commonality among all people, it is our need for a Savior.

LIFE LESSON 14

OBEDIENCE MATTERS: THE FALL OF JERICHO

- **Red Line Verse:** *There are things under the ban in your midst, O Israel; You cannot stand before your enemies until you have removed the things under the ban from your midst.* (Joshua 7:13)

- **Red Line Statement:** God continued faithfully to keep His covenant, but the people struggled with sin, resulting in devastating consequences.

Red Line Connection: Sin has terrible consequences and blocks the flow of God's blessings.

Focal Passage: Joshua 6–7

 Listen Attentively to the Lesson

1. Tell the story of Joshua 6–7 in your own words.

    Context: The focus of these lesson chapters, though detailing Achan's sin in chapter seven, points clearly to the scarlet line of redemption; redemption available to all humanity. In chapter six, we see the story of Rahab, who was saved along with her entire household through contact with God's people. Believing in the witness to God, Rahab lowered a scarlet thread in an opening along the Jericho wall that was about to fall. In God's great orchestration of His redemptive plan, Rahab was transformed from being an enemy of God's people to being part of the ancestral line of the Messiah, Jesus Christ.

2. Ask the small-group members to review the story of Rahab in Joshua 6, including details they remember.

3. Ask the small-group members to reconstruct the story of Achan in Joshua 7, together, including as many details as they can remember. This will be the primary focus of this lesson.

4. Read the passage aloud together from Scripture, confirming the facts of the story. Amend any details suggested by small-group members that did not accurately represent the Scripture.

Investigate the Facts of the Lesson

Use these questions to guide small-group members to investigate the facts of this passage.

1. Who committed the sin? What was the sin (7:19–21)?

    Refer to God's instructions in Joshua 6:18–19. Achan had taken some of the forbidden items from Jericho instead of following God's instructions to destroy everything except the silver, gold, and vessels of bronze and iron that were to be preserved for God's treasury. God called the sin stealing and deception and said that Israel had broken covenant (7:11). See Deuteronomy 6:17 and 7:26 for specific references to the covenant.

2. How were the people to prepare for the day of restoration (7:13)?

    They were to be sanctified. This process was business with God, and it was a holy business. They were to present themselves as a people set apart because they belonged to God.

3. What was the procedure God used to identify the culprit (7:14)?

    God used a narrowing process. First He named the tribe, then the family, next the household, and finally the man who was guilty of sin. Imagine the suspense and intense pressure each man felt under the scrutiny of God, but especially the anxiety that Achan and his family must have felt. Point out to your small group that it was God who called out the offender, not man; God was purging His people from this offense, and He is our Judge.

4. Why did Achan take the forbidden items (7:21)?

    Like Eve, Achan allowed his eyes to linger on what God had forbidden. He looked on the forbidden items and called them "good," using the same word that Eve used to describe the forbidden fruit (Genesis 3:6) and that God used to describe His creation (Genesis 1:12). Sin results when mankind is not satisfied with the "good" that God gives us, and instead man calls "good" what God has called "accursed" (Joshua 6:18 NKJV).

5. What other details do you see in this passage?

   Allow your small group to share other details that stand out to them and discuss the significance of each point.

Find the purpose of the lesson

Use these questions to guide small-group members to discover God's purpose for the passage.

1. Achan buried the stolen items (7:21). Digging the hole, burying the items, and covering them up were three actions — three opportunities to realize how guilty he was before God and repent. When we go to such measures to conceal our sin, are we fooling God? Are we fooling ourselves?

   Nothing can be hidden from God (Hebrews 4:13), but we have the capacity to fool ourselves into thinking that a secret sin is safely hidden from others ("I'll never get caught") or from God ("it's not a big deal; God probably doesn't even care"). Challenge your small group not to focus on how other people fool themselves, but instead to focus on the ways perhaps they have fooled themselves. "Be sure your sin will find you out" (Numbers 32:23).

2. God made the situation very clear: "I will not be with you anymore unless you destroy the things under the ban from your midst... you cannot stand before your enemies until you have removed the things under the ban from your midst" (7:12–13). Have you ever experienced a long-term barrier in your life because of unconfessed sin?

   Allow everyone to respond. Discuss the affects of personal sin, even for a believer. Sometimes in Scripture, God chose to punish people for their sin with one act of judgment, and in other instances such as this scenario, God promises to impose long-term punishment for sin until repentance and restoration have taken place. Encourage each person to consider how important it is to stay clean before God through confession (1 John 1:8–9).

3. Read Joshua 7:11 again. Only one man took of the accursed things, yet God held all of Israel responsible. What does this teach us about how the sin of one affects everyone in the body of Christ (the church)? Have you ever considered how your walk with Christ affects God's interactions with your church?

   The children of Israel were united as a people, experiencing life together. God valued their interconnection and chose to deal with them as one body. Even today, the sin of the individual can certainly affect the life of a church. First Corinthians 12:26–27 teaches that we all suffer when one suffers. Ecclesiastes 9:18 says that "one sinner destroys much good." Encourage your small group to discuss their thoughts on the impact of their walk with Christ on the church body.

4. Did the children of Israel have the right to exercise this death penalty on Achan and his family? Should God's people today take action against sin within the body?

   Joshua and the people had the right and obligation to execute this judgment; God had instructed them to do so under penalty of staying "doomed to destruction" (7:12 NKJV). Just as Joshua followed God's leadership in dealing with Achan, today's church must also follow God's directives for church discipline found in Scripture. First Corinthians 5:1–13 contains Paul's instructions on dealing with an unrepentant sinner in the church.

5. What other truths from this passage stand out to you? What else can we learn about God or learn about being a follower of Christ?

   Allow everyone to respond. Share any other points of spiritual growth that the Holy Spirit brings to your attention.

Experience the Truth of the Lesson
Use these questions to guide small-group members to allow God's transformational truths to reshape their hearts and minds.

1. Achan admitted his sin (7:20), but God knew Achan's heart didn't receive his admission as confession and repentance. How do you guard your heart against taking sin lightly as a Christian, knowing that Christ has paid your sin debt on the Cross?

   Encourage your small-group members to answer the question from their own lives. Challenge them to spend time with God in confession and repentance.

2. Achan and his family were taken to the Valley of Achor for the execution of their death sentence (7:24–26). In Hosea 2:15, God spoke of restoration for His unfaithful people: "I will give her . . . the Valley of Achor as a door of hope."

   a. How did God's judgment usher Israel to the door of hope? What about hope for us today?

      When Achan and his family were put to death, God's wrath was satisfied and He restored His hand of favor to the children of Israel. Today, God brings us to the door of hope through the Cross, where God's wrath was satisfied in the sacrificial death of Jesus Christ.

   b. Imagine this scene taking place in the Valley of Achor. Are you standing with Joshua, crouching with Achan, or casually observing from afar?

      Encourage each person to share how he or she connects with this story from Scripture.

   c. The stone heap (7:26) would remind generations to come of what God had done that day. Have you been fully restored by God? Have your sins been forgiven?

Take time to remember. Encourage group members to remember what we call in our culture milestones of our lives when God restored them and brought them to a new place of nearness to Him.

Between the Lines: Truth Points

Transgress (v. 11)—literally, to pass or cross over; overstepping the bounds of a covenant.

Consecrate (v. 13)—to be holy, to dedicate oneself.

Tribes (v. 14)—the twelve units that comprised the Hebrew nation. Each tribe derived from one of the twelve sons of Jacob (also called Israel), thus, the Hebrews were also called the children of Israel.

Achan (v. 18)—Also called *Achar* (1 Chronicles 2:7), his name means "troubler."

Mantle from Shinar (v. 21)—a mantle was a loose-fitting outer garment worn as a robe or tunic; Shinar was the place where the tower of Babel was built (Genesis 11:2).

Shekel (v. 21)—weight of about four-tenths of an ounce

Achor (v. 24)—trouble

You are but a poor soldier of Christ if you think you can overcome without fighting, and suppose you can have the crown without the conflict.   JOHN CHRYSOSTOM

GOD BEARS WITH HIS PEOPLE: THE JUDGES

Red Line Verse: *Yet they did not listen to their judges, for they played the harlot after other gods and bowed themselves down to them. They turned aside quickly from the way in which their fathers had walked in obeying the commandments of the LORD; they did not do as their fathers.* (Judges 2:17)

Red Line Statement: God's people broke their covenant with God by committing idolatry and intermingling with wicked nations, yet God was still merciful to send godly leaders to help His people overcome their enemies.

Red Line Connection: Mankind is unfaithful, yet God is faithful. Even though we don't deserve His love and protection, God is patient with His people and redemption is His great gift.

Focal Passage: Judges 2:7–19

 Listen Attentively to the Lesson

1. Tell the story of Judges 2:7–19 in your own words.

   Context: The days of Joshua were fruitful for the children of Israel. "So the LORD gave Israel all the land which He had sworn to give to their fathers, and they possessed it and lived in it. And the LORD gave them rest on every side, according to all that He had sworn to their fathers, and no one of all their enemies stood before them; the LORD gave all their enemies into their hand.

Not one of the good promises which the LORD had made to the house of Israel failed; all came to pass" (Joshua 21:43–45). As Joshua approached death, he charged the people to hold fast to the Lord. He reminded them of all God had done for them, and challenged them, "Now, therefore, fear the LORD and serve Him in sincerity and truth; and put away the gods which your fathers served beyond the River and in Egypt, and serve the LORD" (Joshua 24:14). The people vowed to serve God (Joshua 24:16–18, 21), but Joshua warned them, "If you forsake the LORD and serve foreign gods, then He will turn and do you harm and consume you after He has done good to you" (Joshua 24:20).

2. Ask the small-group members to reconstruct the story of Judges 2:7–19 together, including as many details as they can remember.

3. Read the passage aloud together from Scripture, confirming the facts of the story. Amend any details suggested by small-group members that did not accurately represent the Scripture.

Investigate the Facts of the Lesson

Use these questions to guide small-group members to investigate the facts of this passage.

1. When did the unfaithfulness begin among the children of Israel (Judges 2:7–11)?

After Joshua and the elders who witnessed "all the great work of the LORD" had died (v. 7), the next generation began worshipping false gods. This new generation had a God-fearing heritage, but they hadn't been eyewitnesses of the mighty works of God like the previous generation (v. 7).

2. God had warned the children of Israel what would result if they didn't obey the covenant (Leviticus 26:14–39; Deuteronomy 28:15–68). What judgment came upon the Hebrews, just as the LORD had spoken and as the LORD had sworn to them (Judges 2:15)?

   Their resources were taken from them, they were sold to become slaves to their enemies, and they were powerless against their enemies (v. 14).

3. What was God's merciful manner of assisting the children of Israel during this difficult time in their history (vv. 16, 18)?

   God raised up and worked through judges to deliver the Hebrews from their enemies.

4. What other details do you see in this passage?

   Allow your small group to share other details that stand out to them and discuss the significance of each point.

Find the purpose of the lesson

Use these questions to guide small-group members to discover God's purpose for the passage.

1. The generation that began to worship false gods did not know the LORD, nor the work which He had done for Israel (v. 10). What does their lack of knowledge tell us about the leaders that helped shape this generation? What warning should

parents glean from this passage? What does this passage say to leaders in the church today?

The Israelite parents and leaders were unsuccessful in transferring their faith to the next generation. Encourage your small group to discuss the importance of parents rearing their children to know the Lord and the faith heritage of their family, and of church leaders preparing the next generation of leaders to follow God's statutes.

2. Because they forsook God and worshipped idols, the Hebrews were plundered, enslaved, and rendered powerless before their enemies. They couldn't seem to learn from their sufferings. Think about your life. Have you ever found yourself plundered by the world, enslaved by sin or sinful people, or powerless against those who wanted to do you harm? How did God rescue you?

   Allow everyone to respond. Be prepared to share your own times of suffering because of sin in your life. Ask your small group if people are always aware of how their sin is causing them to be plundered, enslaved, and weakened. Focus on God's redemption.

3. God was moved to pity for Israel because of their anguish (v. 18), though they had brought their sorrows upon themselves. How does God's response to the Hebrews in this passage compare to Jesus' response to the Hebrews in Matthew 9:36?

   Jesus was moved with compassion for the scattered people who were wandering about like sheep with no shepherd. God had sent Jesus to the "scattered sheep" to deliver them from their sins, even though they rejected Jesus Christ as Lord. Likewise, in the Book of Judges we see God sending judges to deliver His people, though they were rejecting Him as God.

4. God described Israel's idolatry as playing the harlot (v. 17). They broke covenant with God by going after "other loves." What are

the other loves that Christians are tempted to go after today? What (or who) competes with God to be the great love of your life?

As your small group discusses the distracting loves of modern society, you may choose to reference 2 Timothy 3:2–4, where Paul writes of the love of self, money, and pleasure.

5. God was merciful to the children of Israel, yet their sin provoked Him to anger (vv. 12, 14). When you think about your sin, do you find it easier to accept God's mercy as He spares you from the full consequences of your sin, or do you dwell more on God's righteous anger? Why is it important to understand both God's mercy and also His righteous anger?

    Encourage personal responses. Guide your small group to embrace the full identity of God; He is the One who is fully justified to be angry with our sin because He is the Holy Creator and One without sin. Yet He loves mankind so much that He chooses to show compassion toward us. Praise God for all of who He is!

6. What other truths from this passage stand out to you? What else can we learn about God or learn about being a follower of Christ?

    Allow everyone to respond. Share any other points of spiritual growth that the Holy Spirit brings to your attention.

Experience the Truth of the Lesson

Use these questions to guide small-group members to allow God's transformational truths to reshape their hearts and minds.

1. We joyfully think of how God keeps His word when we're reaping benefits from His promises, yet in Judges 2 the Israelites struggled in their sin because God kept the word of warning He

had given them if they chose to worship idols. Knowing God always keeps His word, how does John 8:23 motivate you?

Encourage your small group to make a specific response to John 8:23 and how it will affect their focus for the coming week.

2. God's delivery through the judges didn't move the Israelites toward love for or loyalty to God; they did not abandon their practices or their ways (v. 19). They were too stubborn to bow the knee to their Lord and Maker. What is the habit, grudge, or bad attitude that you identify in yourself that you're stubbornly refusing to abandon? Will you finally bow the knee before God and abandon that practice?

Encourage everyone to release that "stubborn way" the Holy Spirit brings to their minds.

3. The children of Israel had turned to idols. God provided times of deliverance through the judges, but despite God's mercy, Judges 2:17 tells us that the people didn't listen to the judges. The Hebrew people were consistently inconsistent (v. 19). Read Revelation 3:15–17. According to Jesus, what causes inconsistency? How will you battle inconsistency in your walk with Christ?

When we feel secure because our circumstances are good, we can be tempted to slip away from God, not remembering how dependant we are upon God in all things. When we realize how truly wretched we are in our sin, our gratitude to the Savior will help us stay consistent in our walk with Christ.

Between the Lines: Truth Points

Gathered to their fathers (v. 10) — died.

Baals (v. 11) — Baal was worshipped as the supreme Canaanite god and considered the god of fertility.

Ashtoreths (v. 13) — Ashtoreth was a Canaanite godess of love, war, and fertility; from Canaanite mythology, it appears that Ashtoreth was the spouse of Baal.

Distressed (v. 15) — the word in the Hebrew gives the idea of being straightened, narrowed, as if causing anxiety because the path is too narrow to provide any way of escape.

> *An exalted view of God brings a clear view of sin and a realistic view of self.*
> HENRY BLACKABY

LIFE LESSON 16

God Blesses the Faithful: Ruth

● **Red Line Verses:** *He saved us, not on the basis of deeds which we have done in righteousness, but according to His mercy, by the washing of regeneration and renewing by the Holy Spirit, whom He poured out upon us richly through Jesus Christ our Savior.* (Titus 3:5–6)

● **Red Line Statement:** While God had chosen the children of Israel as His own special people, God also redeemed others who turned to Him in faith.

● **Red Line Connection:** Ruth is a picture of God's grace and redemption. She was born an enemy of God, but she turned to God and He embraced her, redeeming her and offering her a new life.

● **Focal Passage:** Ruth 1

 Listen Attentively to the Lesson

1. Tell the story of Ruth 1 in your own words.

   Context: Elimelech and Naomi lived in the era of the judges (v. 1), which was a tumultuous time for the Hebrew people. "In those days there was no king in Israel; every man did what was right in his own eyes" (Judges 17:6). God brought judgment upon His people because of their rebellion, and famine hit their land (v. 1). Elimelech and Naomi wandered into the enemy territory of Moab seeking food and suffered loss in this foreign land. However, the story of Ruth is one of God's great mercy and His redemption. Ruth the Moabitess found grace in the eyes of God and was given a special honor in God's story that we're tracing on the *thin red line*.

2. Ask the small-group members to reconstruct the story of Ruth 1 together, including as many details as they can remember.

3. Read the passage aloud together from Scripture, confirming the facts of the story. Amend any details suggested by small-group members that did not accurately represent the Scripture.

 Investigate the Facts of the Lesson

Use these questions to guide small-group members to investigate the facts of this passage.

1. Why did Elimelech and Naomi leave Bethlehem for Moab (v. 1)? Why did Naomi return (v. 6)?

   They left Bethlehem because of famine in this town whose name ironically means "house of bread." They were looking in the outside world among God's enemies to have their needs met, instead of fully looking to God (Matthew 6:24–33). Naomi returned to Bethlehem from Moab ten years later because she heard that God had restored bread to Bethlehem.

2. The Moabites were the descendants of Lot (Genesis 19:30–38). Read Deuteronomy 23:3, 6. What had God instructed concerning the Moabites? How did the two sons dishonor God with their life choices in Moab (Ruth 1:4)?

   The sons took foreign wives of a people whom God would not even permit into the assembly of the Lord. Historically, many of the problems the children of Israel experienced were linked to their intermarriage with other nations, which God had forbidden (Deuteronomy 7:3; Joshua 23:12–13). Ezra 9:1–4 makes clear God's disdain for intermarriage with the Moabites.

3. When Naomi talked with Ruth and Orpah about her return to Bethlehem, what did Naomi encourage them to do (Ruth 1:8–15)? As a small group discuss Naomi's instructions to Ruth.

   Naomi encouraged them to return to their birth families (v. 8) and implied they should remarry (v. 9). She encouraged them to turn around on the road and return to Moab (vv. 11,12). After Orpah left, Naomi encouraged Ruth to follow Orpah back to Moab, but note she didn't instruct Ruth to return to false gods; she only stated that this was the choice Orpah had made (v. 15).

4. Back in Bethlehem, Naomi said, "The LORD has witnessed against me" (v. 21). Why would Naomi feel that her afflictions were part of God's judgment against her?

   Perhaps Naomi felt convicted about traveling to Moab for food and living among the enemies of God, or she may have felt conviction that her sons had married Moabite women on her watch. Perhaps Naomi had other sin issues we're not told about in Scripture. Naomi may have simply assumed, as many erroneously did in that culture, that any bad circumstance a person experiences is punishment from God.

   Lead your small group to discuss a believer's need for discernment when he or she experiences personal hardships. How does God want us to respond to trials?

5. Think about God's timing in this story. What was happening in community life in Bethlehem when Naomi and Ruth returned (v. 22)?

   God brought them back at barley harvest time. Share that this timing set up the scenario for Ruth to meet Boaz, the wealthy landowner who would be

33

her kinsman redeemer and second husband. Ruth met Boaz while gleaning in his fields at the time of harvest (Ruth 2).

6. What other details do you see in this passage?

Allow your small group to share other details that stand out to them and discuss the significance of each point.

Find the purpose of the lesson

Use these questions to guide small-group members to discover God's purpose for the passage.

1. Naomi told her friends not to call her Naomi, a name meaning "pleasant," but to call her Mara, which means "bitter" (vv. 19–21). Have you ever struggled with bitterness because of hardship in your life? How does a believer overcome bitterness?

Encourage everyone to be transparent with one another; we all experience hardships, whether because of sin or due to the fallen state of this world. In moments of pain or loss, we each must choose whether to trust God or become bitter. Job 1:21 and 2:9–10 lend perspective to this discussion and challenge us to fully accept God's authority in our lives.

2. Examine Ruth's words in Ruth 1:16–17. Was Ruth choosing God only out of loyalty to Naomi? Is it possible to have a relationship with God out of loyalty to a friend or family member?

Ruth's love for Naomi is evident, and Ruth did indeed pledge her loyalty to Naomi (v. 17). However, Ruth's declaration reveals that she had thought well beyond a duty to care for her mother-in-law. Ruth not only abandoned Moab by crossing its borders, but she fully disowned her people. Ruth was embracing Naomi, the Israelite people, and the Israelites's God. Had Ruth only desired to please Naomi, nothing more, Ruth's pagan ways would have shown themselves in time. Ruth was faithful to Naomi and to God.

This discussion is an important opportunity for your small group to examine what has unfortunately become a familiar story today — two people joining together to become a family unit with one person yielding to the other's Christian beliefs only to keep peace in the home. Jesus said that a person must be born again to receive the kingdom of heaven (John 3:3); living with a Christian and adopting his or her ideas does not create the life transformation that only occurs through the power of the Holy Spirit (Titus 3:5). Ask the Holy Spirit to guide your words so that you are sensitive as well as plainly understood by any small-group members who consider themselves Christians by "choice" but have never experienced true regeneration.

3. The entirety of Ruth's story includes her marriage to Boaz, a close relative of Elimelech. Boaz chose to be the kinsman redeemer (the close male relative who married the widow). As redeemer, Boaz purchased all that was Elimelech's, Chilion's, and Mahlon's from Naomi (Ruth 4:9–10). He paid a great price to make Ruth his bride, and he did so with joy because he loved her (Ruth 2–3). How is the kinsman redeemer a picture of our redemption in Christ?

   We are the bride of Christ (Romans 7:4), and we have been bought with a price (1 Corinthians 6:20). We have been redeemed by the great price of the blood of Jesus because He has chosen to love us and receive us as His special bride. (See "Sons in my womb" under Truth Points.)

4. God instructed the Israelites in Deuteronomy 23:6, "You shall never seek (the Moabites's) peace or their prosperity all your days," yet God gave the Moabitess Ruth peace and prosperity as a God-fearer. The Book of Ruth explains how she married Boaz, a wealthy, God-fearing man who loved her and, most importantly, how Ruth became a member of the lineage of King David (4:22) and King Jesus (Matthew 1:1–17, especially v. 5). How is

Ruth's life a picture of God's grace and salvation? How does her experience compare to what we experience when we come to Christ?

Christians have much in common with Ruth. She used to be an enemy of God by birth, just as we were also enemies of God, born with a sin nature, and separated from Him because of our sin (Colossians 1:21). When Ruth turned away from her past and accepted God as her personal Lord, He gave Ruth a new life; we also experience new life in Christ when we turn from our sins and accept Jesus as Lord. Ruth became a blessed and embraced member of God's family, being grafted into God's faith family, just as we experience adoption (Galatians 4:5) through Christ. God extended to her the full measure of His love by allowing her to be in the lineage of the Messiah. We receive the fullness of Christ (John 1:16).

36

5. What other truths from this passage stand out to you? What else can we learn about God or learn about being a follower of Christ?

    Allow everyone to respond. Share any other points of spiritual growth that the Holy Spirit brings to your attention.

Experience the Truth of the Lesson

Use these questions to guide small-group members to explore God's transformational truths.

1. Because Ruth was a Moabitess, it's quite possible that Naomi, Elimelech, and their two sons were her only witnesses in Moab of the one true God. Regardless of Naomi's shortcomings, Ruth was drawn to Naomi's belief system and her God. Who are the people in your life who receive a gospel witness through you? Does your walk with Christ compel others to know Him?

    Allow everyone to respond. Be prepared to share from your own experiences.

2. Ruth sought and found refuge by trusting in God (Ruth 2:12). Her life story testifies that she was a woman who had been transformed by God. How has God transformed your life?

Be prepared to share from your own experiences. Encourage each person to search carefully and prayerfully for a true conversion experience in his or her life.

3. Ruth wasn't one of God's chosen people by birth, and neither is most of the world. What does it mean to you to know that God offers redemption to all who believe (Romans 1:16)?

Spend time praising God for His grace. (A true "Jew" is described in Romans 2:29.)

Between the Lines: Truth Points

Moab—the land of the Moabites, who were a people stemming from Lot's incestuous relations with his oldest daughter (Genesis 19:30–37)

Ephrathites (v. 2)—People of Ephrathah, a place identified with Bethlehem (Genesis 35:19, Micah 5:2)

Sons in my womb (v. 11)—Naomi had no other sons to offer as husbands to Orpah and Ruth. In Deuteronomy 25:5–6, the law required that if brothers lived together, a dead man's brother was to wed the widow if she had no son. Once they had a son, they were to name the child after the dead brother. By accomplishing this role, the living brother (called the kinsman) redeemed the deceased brother's name and inheritance. Other close relatives were also eligible to serve in the various duties of a kinsman.

He wants us to have a faith that does not complain while waiting, but rejoices because we know our times are in His hands — nail-scarred hands that labor for our highest good.

KAY ARTHUR

A Young and Faithful Servant: Samuel Hears from God

- **Red Line Verse:** *Samuel grew and the LORD was with him and let none of his words fail.* (1 Samuel 3:19)

- **Red Line Statement:** God provided prophets and priests to lead and guide His people into righteousness.

- **Red Line Connection:** The prophets God appointed provided great spiritual leadership to the Israelites and their leaders. They offered guidance and also pointed the Israelites to look toward their future King of kings.

- **Focal Passage:** 1 Samuel 3

 Listen Attentively to the Lesson

1. Tell the story of 1 Samuel 3 in your own words.

    Context: The priest Eli had wicked sons who served as priests but did not know the Lord (1 Samuel 2:12–17, 22), and God held Eli responsible for indulging his sons in their evil behavior (2:29). God pronounced judgment against Eli and his household and promised to raise up a faithful priest (2:31–36).

    God had already set a plan in motion to provide His people with a God-fearing priest. The Hebrew woman Hannah was barren and pled with the Lord for a son, promising to dedicate the child to God if He would answer her prayer (1:11). God gave Hannah a son, Samuel, whose name means "the name is El" (God) (1:20). After Hannah weaned Samuel, she took him to live as a servant of God under the care of Eli (1:24–28).

Samuel's ministry marked a turning point in the history of the Israelites. He was their last judge before the era of the kings (7:16, 8:1–5).

2. Ask the small-group members to reconstruct the story of 1 Samuel 3 together, including as many details as they can remember.

3. Read the passage aloud together from Scripture, confirming the facts of the story. Amend any details suggested by small-group members that did not accurately represent the Scripture.

Investigate the Facts of the Lesson

Use these questions to guide small-group members to investigate the facts of this passage.

1. What was the spiritual climate during the early days of Samuel's childhood (1 Samuel 3:1)?

   The people rarely heard a word from God. Samuel was born during the era of the judges, and it was generally a time of spiritual darkness (Judges 17:6). The wicked behaviors of Eli's sons, acting immorally as priests (1 Samuel 2:12–17,22), only exasperated the people's struggles.

2. Why did Samuel think that Eli was calling him in the night (1 Samuel 3:7)?

   Samuel didn't know the Lord personally, nor had he been exposed to God's words or voice. Until this point in his young life, Samuel had been serving in the Tabernacle, but not yet serving God in a personal manner through a relationship with Him.

3. How was God blessing His people by calling Samuel to be a prophet?

God's people are nourished by God's Word, and the people would be greatly blessed to hear from God through the prophet. The people were suffering under a lack of spiritual leadership because of Eli's sons and Eli's indulgence of them. Samuel's emergence as a prophet and priest let the Israelites know that God was still mindful of them.

4. What other details do you see in this passage?

Allow your small group to share other details that stand out to them and discuss the significance of each point.

Find the purpose of the lesson

Use these questions to guide small-group members to discover God's purpose for the passage.

1. Before Samuel realized it was the Lord who was calling him, he rose from his bed and ran to Eli's side three times. Samuel didn't complain about the inconvenience of being called out of his rest. We see a willingness within Samuel to be a servant. What are the marks of a willing servant of God? How do you respond when God calls you out of a time of rest?

Some possible answers include immediate and complete obedience, humility, joy in service, unwavering loyalty, unquestioning faith in the Master, a desire for God to receive all glory, a desire for the kingdom of God to be blessed, and thankfulness. Encourage everyone to discuss how God gives us seasons of rest, followed by times of action and ministry.

2. Samuel was already serving in the Tabernacle before God spoke to Him, but after the vision, life changed for Samuel. What happens to a person who is transformed from being one who does tasks in God's house to being one who knows God personally?

Any person can be in church and even participate in service within the church, learning more about God and the church by observing others (in Samuel's case, observing Eli). However, when a person becomes a Christian, he or she hears from God personally. A Christian's ministry is shaped by God, and God can do great things through service done in Jesus' name. Encourage your small-group members to talk about how they have experienced this for themselves, as they went from being church attendees to being Christians.

3. God called Samuel by name. What does John 10:3 teach us about how God speaks to His children? When have you heard God speak specifically to you?

John 10:3 teaches us that Christ calls His sheep by name. Not only does God call by name those who are called into vocational ministry like Samuel, but God also calls by name every sheep of Christ. Encourage group members to share about a time when God spoke specifically to them.

4. Samuel was young when God called him and gave him this vision. Does God still call young people today? Are you open to the ability of children and youth to serve in ministry and worship?

Encourage your small group to examine their thinking about the ministry of young people. Challenge members to consider how they can encourage the ministry of the young people of your church, and how they can make a positive impact in the lives of children and youth who want to serve the Lord now, even before they reach adulthood.

5. Becoming a prophet as a youth may have been very challenging for Samuel. Have you ever felt that a season of your life was not

a good or convenient time to serve God? Seasons of life can be based on age, life circumstances, or stages of family life.

Encourage members to share any assumptions they have made about why they can't serve God in particular ministries because of a season of life. Remind everyone that God's call trumps our beliefs about our seasons of life.

6. God gave Samuel a very difficult message concerning Eli. Does God still ask His servants to speak difficult words to people who are not exhibiting obedient lifestyles before Him? God continues to use His people to be His mouthpiece.

   Ask your small group if anyone can share a testimony about a time God used him or her to encourage someone to turn toward God and away from sin. Remind everyone how important it was that Samuel told the whole truth to Eli, nothing more and nothing less, giving us the example of only speaking God's message to edify others.

43

7. God told Samuel that the sacrifices and offerings of Eli and his sons would not be accepted for the atonement of their sins (1 Samuel 3:14). They were willfully disobeying God and unrepentant. What does God desire of His people more than an act of sacrifice?

   We no longer participate in the sacrificial system because Jesus is our perfect sacrifice who died for the atonement of our sins. However, God continues to look at the heart of the sinner when it comes to the matter of repentance. It was not the ritual of sacrificing an animal that satisfied God in the Old Testament if the individual's heart was not broken and contrite over sin. Similarly, God examines our hearts as we come to Him seeking forgiveness of our sins, as Christ taught us to pray (Matthew 6:12). The following verses offer insight into what God desires more than sacrifice: Proverbs 15:8; Isaiah 1:11–17; Hosea 6:6; and Micah 6:8. Samuel learned this lesson all too well from watching Eli's mistakes, and Samuel himself spoke on this matter in 1 Samuel 15:22.

8. What other truths from this passage stand out to you? What else can we learn about God or learn about being a follower of Christ?

    Allow everyone to respond. Share any other points of spiritual growth that the Holy Spirit brings to your attention.

Experience the Truth of the Lesson

Use these questions to guide small-group members to allow God's transformational truths to reshape their hearts and minds.

1. Just as Eli's sons had brought shame in people's eyes concerning the role of the priest, even today there are some who profess Christianity who cause people to think less of Christians because of their sinful behavior. Think about how God used Samuel to restore honor to the priesthood. Are you available for God to use to bring honor to the name "Christian"?

    The title of Christian is an honor because we represent Jesus Christ. Encourage small group members to make a personal examination of their lifestyles and to consider prayerfully if Christ is glorified and the title of Christian is upheld by their words, actions, and values.

2. If God were to call upon you today to be His messenger, are you ready to obey? Are you seeking to do God's will?

    As your small group responds, remind everyone that Jesus has already called upon each of us to be His messengers: "Therefore, we are ambassadors for Christ, as though God were making an appeal through us; we beg you on behalf of Christ, be reconciled to God" (2 Corinthians 5:20). Encourage your small group to pray about how they can be more available to God to be His messengers of truth.

Between the Lines: Truth Points

Lamp of God (v. 3)—the seven-branched golden candlestick positioned in the Holy Place before the veil, left of the golden altar of incense (Exodus 25:31–40; 27:20–21; 37:17–24)

Ark of God (1 Samuel 3:3)—the Ark of the Covenant. God originally instructed that it be built to hold the Ten Commandments (Deuteronomy 10:1–5).

Shall not be atoned for by sacrifice (v. 14)—In Numbers 15:30, God warned that willful sinners were to be cut off from the assembly.

Let none of his words fail (v. 19)—First Samuel 9:6 affirms that Samuel was known as one whose prophetic words came to pass.

Shiloh (v. 21)—a city positioned about 30 miles north of Jerusalem. Shiloh was the location of Israel's Tabernacle (Joshua 18:1), and thus a hub of religious activity.

> *You must never sacrifice your relationship with God for the sake of a relationship with another person.* CHARLES STANLEY

MORTAL MONARCHS

The period of the kings is a sordid time in Israel's history. Great men like David left a legacy that inspires us all to be men and women after God's own heart, but the failures of lesser men such as King Saul make us feel weary of weak men who lead us poorly.

Earthly kings and political figures have the ability to inspire or discourage the masses, but no mortal monarch can do what King Jesus has accomplished: no earthly king can truly set us free. As you study the accomplishments and failures of some of Israel's most notable kings, celebrate the many ways that God was pointing His people to the coming King. Jesus is our King, and He shall reign forever. How glorious to be known and loved by the King of kings, He who has redeemed all His people.

LIFE LESSON 18

MISUSE OF GOD'S BLESSING:
THE DEMISE OF KING SAUL

Red Line Verse: *Much more then, being now justified by his blood, we shall be saved from wrath through him.* (Romans 5:9 NKJV)

Red Line Statement: God provided a means for the people to receive forgiveness of their sins through the sacrificial system, and God required that His plan be followed exactly.

Red Line Connection: God has provided redemption for mankind through Jesus Christ, and God requires that all people go through Jesus Christ and Him alone for forgiveness of sin.

Focal Passage: 1 Samuel 13:1–14

 Listen Attentively to the Lesson

1. Tell the story of 1 Samuel 13:1–14 in your own words.

Context: The prophet and priest Samuel was aging, and his sons were not godly priests. The people of Israel rose up and demanded that Samuel give them a king so they could be like the other nations, having someone to judge them and fight their battles (1 Samuel 8:5, 20). Samuel was angry, but God said, "Listen to the voice of the people in regard to all that they say to you, for they have not rejected you, but they have rejected Me from being king over them. Like all the deeds which they have done since the day that I brought them up from Egypt even to this day — in that they have forsaken Me and served other gods — so they are doing to you also. Now then, listen to their voice; however, you shall solemnly warn them and tell them of the procedure of the king who will reign over them" (8:7–9). Saul of the tribe of Benjamin was chosen by God to be Israel's first king. Samuel anointed Saul (10:1), and proclaimed him to be God's chosen king before the people. The day must have been bittersweet for Israel, because Samuel once again described Israel's demand for a king as a rejection of God (10:19).

Saul's first act as king established Saul in the hearts of the people. The Ammonites (descendants of Lot, Genesis 19:38) encamped around Jabesh-Gilead ready to attack. The Israelites of Jabesh were willing to enslave themselves to the Ammonites in exchange for a peace covenant, but the Ammonites's demands were humiliating and devastating—the right eye of every Israelite in Jabesh was to be gouged out (1 Samuel 11:1–2). Saul rallied a great army and utterly defeated the Ammonites, giving God the glory and saying that "today the LORD has accomplished deliverance in Israel" (11:13).

Despite Israel's rejection of God by demanding a king, God was gracious and merciful. "The LORD will not abandon His people on account of His great name, because the LORD has been pleased to make you a people for Himself" (12:22). God offered the people the opportunity to remain in His will if they would serve and obey Him (12:14). Difficult days were ahead for Israel, but God would remain faithful to His beloved people.

49

2. Ask the small-group members to reconstruct the story of 1 Samuel 13:1–14 together, including as many details as they can remember.

3. Read the passage aloud together from Scripture, confirming the facts of the story. Amend any details suggested by small-group members that did not accurately represent the Scripture.

Investigate the Facts of the Lesson
Use these questions to guide small-group members to investigate the facts of this passage.

1. Saul's son Jonathan struck a blow to the Philistines when he attacked the garrison at Geba. What did Saul do next (1 Samuel 13:3)? What was Saul attempting to do?

Saul began the process of driving out the Philistines from Canaan. The land rightfully belonged in Saul's kingdom because the land had been promised to the Hebrews. Saul was calling the people to Gilgal to prepare for more military offenses against the Philistines.

2. What did the Israelites hear about happenings in Geba (v. 4)? What was their perspective?

   The people credited Saul, not Jonathan, for attacking the garrison. Note that the Israelites took the attack as a cause for the Philistines to now view them as an abomination and perhaps be more punitive toward them. Scripture does not record any jubilation among the Israelites because their enemies were being driven from the land.

3. Why was it a sin for Saul to offer the burnt offering?

   After the Israelites escaped Egypt, God laid out a detailed sacrificial system. Chapters one to seven of Leviticus give great detail about this system. Priests were supposed to play an integral part in the burnt offering (Leviticus 1, 6:8–13) as well as the peace offering (Leviticus 3, 7:11–21). See Numbers 18:7.

4. What other details do you see in this passage?

   Allow your small group to share other details that stand out to them and discuss the significance of each point.

Find the purpose of the lesson

   Use these questions to guide small-group members to discover God's purpose for the passage.

1. When Samuel arrived, what did he ask Saul (v. 11)? With Samuel's question and Saul's excuses, how is this conversation

similar to what happened when God confronted Adam and Eve's sin (Genesis 3:12–13)? How is this situation similar to how God interacts in your life when you sin?

Samuel asked Saul what he had done, just as God asked the woman. Like Saul, Adam and Eve both made excuses and blamed others for their sin (Genesis 3:12–13). We also face the temptation to make excuses. Share 1 John 1:8–9 with your small group. We deceive ourselves when we think other people's sins or bad circumstances justify our poor decisions. Answering the question, "What have you done?" is our opportunity to confess our sins before God, which is necessary for forgiveness.

2. Consider Saul's excuses for offering the burnt offering himself (vv. 11–12). What is at the heart of each excuse? Which excuse can you relate to the most?

Saul tried to justify his actions by describing a bleak situation that he felt warranted taking matters into his own hands. "Desperate times call for desperate measures" was his claim. First he mentioned that the Israelites were scattering. Sometimes when the people around us don't rise to the occasion and appear to be failing us, we are tempted to act rashly out of desperation. Second, Saul implied that Samuel had let him down with a late arrival. Sometimes when we sense that time is running out for a solution (a bill is now due, a child's disobedience is worsening dramatically, etc.), we are tempted to jump ahead of God to make our own solution. Third, Saul felt the pressure of his enemies gathered in great numbers against him in Michmash, less than 20 miles away from Gilgal. Most of us can relate, having experienced fear when enemies have threatened our safety.

Allow your small group to share how they relate to Saul's excuses. Each excuse resulted from Saul's lack of faith. Saul made his decision based on circumstances. Share Hebrews 11:6 and encourage everyone to consider how faith overcomes excuses.

3. Saul said he "forced himself" (v. 12) or "felt compelled" (v. 12 NKJV) to offer the burnt offering because he didn't want to go to battle without having first asked God for His blessing. Does God ever put us in situations that force us to go against His commandments?

James 1:13–14 teaches that God doesn't lead us into sin. In light of this obvious answer, ask your small group to consider why people so often say, "I know it's wrong, but…"

4. Samuel gave Saul a seven-day window for his arrival (v. 8), but Samuel delayed his arrival on the scene. Why does God test our patience? How is God working in this area of your life?

God calls upon His people to be patient for His deliverance. Our patience is a display of our faith, and the waiting process builds our faith and causes us to rely upon the Lord. References regarding waiting upon the Lord include: Psalm 33:20, 37:7, 130:6; Lamentations 3:25. Encourage everyone to share his or her testimony of waiting upon the Lord.

5. What other truths from this passage stand out to you? What else can we learn about God or learn about being a follower of Christ?

Allow everyone to respond. Share any other points of spiritual growth that the Holy Spirit brings to your attention.

Experience the Truth of the Lesson

Use these questions to guide small-group members to allow God's transformational truths to reshape their hearts and minds.

1. How were Saul's actions a misuse of God's blessing? What is the danger today of people misusing God's blessing?

The Old Testament sacrificial system was God's method to allow people to receive forgiveness of their sins (Numbers 18:5). Saul was trying to gain God's forgiveness and blessing his own way, not God's way. The danger today is the same. People without Christ are trying to deal with their sin problems through their own manmade ideas of redemption. Christians may also misuse God's blessing of redemption through Jesus Christ by indulging in sin and taking lightly Christ's sacrifice on the Cross. Share Hebrews 10:26–31 and ask your small group to respond to these strong words of warning.

2. Ecclesiastes 7:8 teaches that the patient in spirit is better than the proud in spirit (NKJV). How is pride the enemy of patience? Can you identify any prideful motivation within yourself that is tempting you to take matters into your own hands?

   Pride gives us the idea that we can handle our own situations without God's help, and that perhaps we know better than God. Pride can also cause us to feel pressured to make something happen in our lives because we don't want to be embarrassed in front of others while we wait for a job, wait for God to fix a problem, wait for God to make His will known, etc. Encourage open sharing. Be prepared to share a personal testimony.

3. Saul's sin resulted in great personal loss (vv. 13–14). He apparently was not "a man after (God's) own heart" (v. 14). What is your passion? How is God reshaping you to become a person after God's own heart?

   Encourage each person to share. Ask the group to at least answer these questions in their own hearts.

Between the Lines: Truth Points

Michmash and Gibeah (v. 2)—cities in the territory of Benjamin, about 4.5 miles apart.

Garrison (v. 3)—a body of troops occupying a region for its defense. The Philistines had stationed garrisons well within the Hebrews' land of Canaan (1 Samuel 10:5, 13:3; 2 Samuel 23:14).

Geba (v. 3)—located in Benjamin's territory; this land had been designated for the Levites (Joshua 21:13–19).

Philistines (v. 3)—this people group was a constant source of conflict for the Israelites. The Philistines are mentioned as early as Genesis, but the major skirmishes began to happen during the period of the judges of Israel. Canaan, the land God had promised the children of Israel, included the land of the Philistines (Joshua 13:1–3).

Gilgal (v. 4)—means *circle* and may refer to a ring of stone set up as an altar; the exact location of Gilgal is debated, as is the possibility of more than one location known as Gilgal.

Burnt offering (v. 9)—this offering was made for the atonement of sins (Leviticus 1:4). Both the priests and the one bringing the offering had specific roles to play in the blood sacrifice process (Leviticus 1, 6:8–13).

Peace offering (v. 9)—this offering was made as a thanksgiving offering, or a vow or voluntary offering (Leviticus 7:12, 16). Like the burnt offering, both the priests and the one bringing the offering had specific roles to play in the blood sacrifice process (Leviticus 1, 6:8–13).

> *Until we learn to trust God and wait on His timing, we can't*
> *learn the other lessons He wants to teach us, nor can we receive*
> *the blessings He's planned for us.*   WARREN WIERSBE

LIFE LESSON 19

GOD'S POWER ON DISPLAY:
THE BOY AND THE GIANT

- **Red Line Verse:** *The LORD does not deliver by sword or by spear; for the battle is the LORD's.* (1 Samuel 17:47)

- **Red Line Statement:** God raised up for the Israelite people a great king named David who demonstrated that salvation comes in the name of the Lord.

- **Red Line Connection:** David was important in the bloodline of Messiah. Jesus was often called "Son of David" (Matthew 21:15). Just as David called upon the name of the Lord and was saved, God has promised salvation to all who call upon His name (Acts 2:21).

- **Focal Passage:** 1 Samuel 17

 Listen Attentively to the Lesson

1. Tell the story of 1 Samuel 17:20–51 in your own words.

   Context: After God rejected Saul as king over the Israelites, God instructed Samuel to travel to Bethlehem to anoint one of the sons of Jesse to be the next king. David was God's chosen vessel, and when he was anointed, the Spirit of the LORD came mightily upon David from that day forward (1 Samuel 16:13). David would have to wait many years before becoming king, but God was preparing him to be a great shepherd over His people. The Philistines assembled for battle against Israel. Saul responded by encamping his men at the Valley of Elah (17:2). The Philistines and Israelites stood on mountainsides opposite each other, on either side of a valley. Every day for 40 days, the scene was the same. The Philistine champion named Goliath stepped out morning and evening (v. 16) to defy the armies of Israel (v. 10). He called for an Israelite to fight him and for the one-on-one battle to determine which army would serve the other (vv. 8–10). Saul and the Israelite army responded in fear (v. 11, 24).

Jesse sent his son, David, to the battlefield with food provisions (vv. 17–18). David was not only about to walk onto the battlefield, he was about to walk into his God-ordained destiny.

2. Ask the small-group members to reconstruct the story of 1 Samuel 17:20–51 together, including as many details as they can remember.

3. Read the passage aloud together from Scripture, confirming the facts of the story. Amend any details suggested by small-group members that did not accurately represent the Scripture.

Investigate the Facts of the Lesson

Use these questions to guide small-group members to investigate the facts of this passage.

1. What method was Saul using to select an opponent to face Goliath (v. 25)?

Instead of calling the men to faith in God, Saul appealed to each man's greed. He offered riches and a position of power as his son-in-law. In this situation, greed was overpowered by fear in the hearts of Israel's soldiers.

2. What seemed to be in the forefront of David's mind throughout this story (vv. 26, 36, 45–47)?

   David took this battle to be a spiritual matter. He was disgusted that an "uncircumcised Philistine" would dare to defy the armies of the living God. David knew the Israelites were God's special people, and that no one had authority to defy God or His people.

3. What had David experienced in His life that gave Him confidence to face the giant (vv. 34–37)?

   God had allowed David to protect sheep from predators, and David considered the situation with Goliath to be no different, "'since he has taunted the armies of the living God'" (v. 36).

4. Standing behind their champion Goliath, what role did the Philistine army play in this story?

   The Philistine army was much like Israel's army, willing to line up for battle but quite content to let one man (Goliath) fight the battle for them. They had placed their confidence in one man. When Goliath fell, the Philistines fled (v. 51).

5. What other details do you see in this passage?

   Allow your small group to share other details that stand out to them and discuss the significance of each point.

Find the purpose of the lesson

Use these questions to guide small-group members to discover God's purpose for the passage.

1. What could have been motivating Eliab to turn against David (v. 28)? How does Eliab's treatment of David compare to

squabbles that occur within the body of Christ today? What was at the heart of Eliab's accusations?

Possible answers: Eliab may have felt threatened by David's courage because it pointed out his own cowardice. Eliab may have also felt jealousy against David, since he was the oldest son of Jesse but had not been selected as God's anointed one (16:6–7). Similarly, sometimes today's believers squabble because one member is jealous of another's position of authority. Another cause can be an inner fear that a courageous, "on fire" church member will force others to step out of their comfort zones or else feel put to shame. Jealousy and fear can only bring destruction and disunity in the family of God.

Eliab's accusations against David indicated his lack of respect for him. He suggested David was just a shepherd who could barely be trusted with even a few sheep, he had no business showing up at their army encampment, and his motivation for being there wasn't pure. These same accusations are sometimes used today when church members squabble, sending messages like: "you aren't worthy of big responsibilities in the church"; "this is our church, and you don't really belong here"; and "your motivations for wanting to do this ministry aren't pure." How ironic that David first had to engage in a war of words with his brother before facing the real enemy, Goliath. Discuss with your small group how God would have church members encourage one another toward courageous acts in God's name.

2. Consider what Saul said to David (1 Samuel 17:33) and what he offered to him (v. 38) when they discussed David facing the giant. What are the signs that Saul wasn't fully trusting God to fight this battle for the Israelite army? In your life, what signs let you know whether you are trusting in God or trusting in someone else to solve your problems?

Saul told David he was too young and inexperienced to face Goliath. Saul then offered David his suit of armor and gave him a coat of mail and a helmet. Allow your small group to share their thoughts. Worries, doubts, fears, depression, and scheming are only a sampling of how our minds can work when we aren't fully relying on God to meet our every need and bring solutions to our problems.

3. David tried on Saul's armor but decided it wasn't for him (v. 39). How did David show wisdom?

Possible answer: He didn't bow to pressure to enter battle Saul's way or the conventional way. Instead, David went with what he knew. He had gained a confidence in God without the armor, and he didn't change this method because of others' expectations.

4. David approached Goliath with a staff and a sling, and Goliath had contempt for David and his weaponry (vv. 42–43).

a. Read 1 Samuel 17:45. What were Goliath's weapons? What was David's primary weapon?

Goliath had a spear, sword, and javelin, but David's weapon was greatest of all: he was armed with the name of the Lord. Reference David's words in verse 47.

b. Was this a fair fight?

Allow everyone to respond. God's name is powerful above all (Psalms 20:7; 118:10–12; 124:8).

c. When facing opposition, what is your weapon of choice?

Challenge your group for an honest answer. Our human nature is to fight problems with denial, sarcasm, throwing money at a problem, counting on influential people or a spouse to bail us out, shutting down, bickering, lying, or some other human response. Encourage everyone to think about the great privilege of calling on the name of the Lord.

5. Goliath's words had intimidated the entire army of Israel, but David was not backing down from the fight. How does Satan try to intimidate Christians today? Have you ever stood strong in the face of Satan's intimidation? Have you ever backed down from the fight?

    Allow your small group to share. Be prepared to share an experience from your own life. As your group shares, encourage everyone to keep in mind the motivation of David: bringing all glory to God. David didn't take Goliath's words personally. Instead, he saw this threat as an affront to God. David was not motivated by hate, anger, or revenge.

6. What other truths from this passage stand out to you? What else can we learn about God or learn about being a follower of Christ?

    Allow everyone to respond. Share any other points of spiritual growth that the Holy Spirit brings to your attention.

Experience the Truth of the Lesson

Use these questions to guide small-group members to allow God's transformational truths to reshape their hearts and minds.

1. David had the army of Israel behind him, but he faced the giant alone. He was the only man willing to demonstrate the power of God. Are you willing to stand alone for God?

    As everyone shares, remind your small group that we are never truly alone when we stand up for God, because He is with us.

2. Do you believe in the power of God? What happens when God's people believe in the power of God?

    Encourage everyone to consider the possibilities of what God can and will do through His people when we fully trust in His name. Encourage answers to be specific.

3. David called upon the name of the Lord. Read Acts 2:17–21. What is God saying to you about calling on the name of the Lord?

As you prepare for this week's small group, pray that God will work in your small-group members' hearts to stir great courage for God's work and full reliance upon the name of the Lord. As you share this question with your small group, challenge everyone to give a faith response that will take them out of their comfort zones to live for God.

Between the Lines: Truth Points

Jesse (v. 20)—David's father (16:10–11).

Goliath (v. 23)—a Philistine giant who stood nine feet, nine inches tall. He wore a coat of mail weighing 125 pounds and carried a 15-pound spear (17:4–5).

Uncircumcised (v. 26)—circumcision was a sign of the covenant that God made with the Israelite people, beginning with Abraham (Genesis 17:10–14). By calling Goliath uncircumcised, David was pointing out that Goliath and the Philistines were not recipients of God's covenant promises to His people.

Eliab (v. 28)—eldest brother of David (17:13).

Shield-bearer (v. 41)—in this era of warfare, a shield was sometimes so large that a soldier was given the task of steadying a shield for another warrior, who could stand behind this over-sized shield of protection.

We honor God by asking for great things when they are part of His promise. We dishonor Him and cheat ourselves when we ask for molehills where He has offered mountains. VANCE HAVNER

REPENTANCE AND RESTORATION: DAVID

Red Line Verses: *Be gracious to me, O God, according to Your lovingkindness; according to the greatness of Your compassion blot out my transgressions. Wash me thoroughly from my iniquity and cleanse me from my sin.* (Psalm 51:1–2)

Red Line Statement: The sin of God's people brought shame and sorrows upon them, but God's forgiveness of those who repented brought restoration, renewal, and rejoicing.

Red Line Connection: God has consistently displayed a willingness to forgive repentant sinners.

Background Passage: 2 Samuel 11–12:24

Focal Passage: Psalm 51

 Listen Attentively to the Lesson

1. Give the context of Psalm 51 by summarizing King David's sin of adultery and murder, recorded in 2 Samuel 11–12:24. Then share in your own words the cry of David's heart recorded in Psalm 51.

    Context: While David's army was engaging in battle, David stayed in Jerusalem. One evening from his roof David saw a woman bathing, and he sent for her to come to him. Her name was Bathsheba, and her husband was Uriah the Hittite, who was away at war as a member of David's army. David had relations with Bathsheba, and she became pregnant. When David learned that she was with child, he had Uriah brought back from the battlefield. David tried to arrange for Uriah to go home and lie with his wife, even getting Uriah drunk. An honorable man, Uriah refused to enjoy the pleasures of home and spend time with Bathsheba while his comrades were still on the battlefield. David would have to cover his sin another way. David sent a note by Uriah to Joab, David's military commander. David instructed Joab to place Uriah on the frontlines of a heated battle and then withdraw so that Uriah would be killed. Joab obeyed David's orders, and Uriah died in battle. After a time of mourning, Bathsheba became David's wife, and the child was born. The prophet Nathan visited David and spoke on God's behalf, confronting David with his sin. God told David that the newborn child would die, and that much trouble would come to David's household because of this sin. The child was sick for seven days and then died, but God was gracious and allowed David and Bathsheba to conceive another child, Solomon.

2. Ask the small-group members to reconstruct Psalm 51 together, including as many details as they can remember.

3. Read the passage aloud together from Scripture, confirming the facts of the story. Amend any details suggested by small-group members that did not accurately represent the Scripture.

Investigate the Facts of the Lesson

Use these questions to guide small-group members to investigate the facts of this passage.

1. What was David asking God to do for him?

   Possible answer: David was seeking cleansing, forgiveness, restoration, and renewal.

2. In Psalm 51:1–3, David expressed many of the hardships of personal sin. What words did David use to describe what he was feeling?

   Possible answers: "be gracious" (v. 1) indicates he felt helpless in his guilt before God, and undeserving; "blot out my transgressions" (v. 1) indicates he felt the weight of his sin debt; "wash me thoroughly" and "cleanse me" (v. 2) express the dirty/defiled feeling that sin creates; "my sin is ever before me" (v. 3) describes the inescapable nature of guilt.

3. What other details do you see in this passage?

   Allow your small group to share other details that stand out to them and discuss the significance of each point.

 Find the purpose of the lesson

Use these questions to guide small-group members to discover God's purpose for the passage.

1. Examine verse 4. David was broken over his sin, and he was repentant.

   a. If you were able to stay mindful that every sin you commit is a personal sin against God, how would this perspective affect your attitudes and actions?

David had sinned against other people, yet he emphasized that his sin was directly against God. Encourage your small group to think about the temptation to trivialize sin or to justify our actions when we focus on how others have wronged us, how others also sin, etc.

b. David called God blameless as a judge. Have you come to a place in your faith journey where you completely yield to God's authority to judge your life?

When David spoke of God as a blameless judge, he was making a complete admission of guilt. Whatever God deemed to be an appropriate response to David's sin, he knew he was deserving of God's judgment. Ask your small group if they have ever come to God with words like, "God, I know I shouldn't feel this way, but..." What does it mean to have a broken and contrite heart over sin? What does it mean to repent?

2. David longed to be purified and washed whiter than snow (v. 7).

a. How thoroughly is God able to wash our souls?

God forgives us of all our sins when we become Christians, and He remembers our sin no more (Jeremiah 31:34). Refer to Psalm 103:12, Isaiah 38:17, Micah 7:19, Romans 8:1, and Revelation 1:5 for further insights, and spend time praising God for His gifts of mercy and grace. Through Christ's blood, we are thoroughly washed clean. His work is complete.

b. Why do Christians sometimes struggle with feelings of guilt and shame?

David said, "My sin is ever before me" (v. 3). Allow small-group members to share their personal struggles with forgiving themselves or accepting and embracing God's forgiveness. Discuss the need for Holy Spirit

*discernment to differentiate between the conviction of the Holy Spirit when
we need to repent versus the burden of guilt that comes from Satan when he
tries to keep us shackled to that from which Christ has already set us free.
You may also have small-group members who have struggles with sin, just
as Paul described in Romans 7:13–25, and some of them may be feeling the
weight of unconfessed sin in their lives. Remind everyone of the importance
of confession and repentance (Matthew 6:12).*

3. David needed God to "renew a steadfast spirit" in him (v. 10).
   Has sin ever been so heavy in your life that you lost your zeal for
   God? How did God renew that steadfastness for you?

   Allow everyone to share. Be prepared to share your own testimony.

66

4. David asked God to cancel his sin debt and not look on his sins
   anymore (v. 9). Read Jesus' teaching in Matthew 6:14–15. Are
   you practicing this principle? How has God taught you to know
   when you have truly released someone from a trespass?

   *Allow your small group to share. Be ready to share an experience from
   your own life.*

5. David expressed a desire to be able to rejoice again (vv. 8, 12,
   14–15). In the past, how has sin affected your ability to worship?

   *As your small group shares, encourage them to evaluate their enthusiasm
   for worship. Are their hearts rejoicing continually, both in times of corporate
   worship and in everyday life? If the answer is no, challenge them to talk with
   God about any sin issue that may be hindering their worship. God is worthy
   of continual worship, and God's people should indeed rejoice!*

6. If you're a Christian, you have experienced firsthand the wonderful gift of God's forgiveness. Think about what David said he
   intended to do in verse 13. What has God taught you through His

forgiveness that you could teach to someone who does not know Christ as Savior?

This question is a wonderful opportunity to encourage your small-group members to share their testimonies with the group, the same testimony they could share with the lost. For any members struggling to put into words what God has done for them, encourage them to share what their lives were like before Christ, how they came to Christ and experienced forgiveness, and what their lives have been like since coming to Christ.

7. What other truths from this passage stand out to you? What else can we learn about God or learn about being a follower of Christ?

   Allow everyone to respond. Share any other points of spiritual growth that the Holy Spirit brings to your attention.

Experience the Truth of the Lesson

Use these questions to guide small-group members to allow God's transformational truths to reshape their hearts and minds.

1. God desires "truth in the innermost being" (v. 6). As you have been studying the Thin Red Line, what has God shown you about being honest with yourself about your faith walk? About being honest before others? About being honest before God?

   As your small group shares about their faith journeys, encourage an authenticity before others, before God, and within themselves.

2. Without God's forgiveness, we would be overwhelmed with the weight of sin, forced to try to earn God's favor through good works, and consumed with guilt before God with a sin debt we could not pay. Read Romans 4:5–8. Are you blessed?

Allow time for testimonies of God's blessings. Be ready to share your own testimony. Encourage the group to carry themselves as people who have been blessed.

3. Through Jesus, God fulfilled His covenant with David that his house and kingdom would be established forever (2 Samuel 7:12–16). David was prominent in the lineage of Jesus Christ, who was referred to in the Gospels as "Son of David" several times. Jesus even called Himself "the descendant of David" (Revelation 22:16). Why did God bless David? Why does God bless you?

God's grace is amazing. David was a sinner, but he continued to worship and pursue God. Encourage your small group to continue to worship and pursue God, even in times of failure.

Between the Lines: Truth Points

Blot out (v. 1)—to stroke, rub, erase, destroy, or wipe out.

Transgression (v. 1)—revolt or rebellion.

Iniquity (v. 2)—an offense against God's law. The usage of the word includes the sin, God's judgment of the sin, and the punishment for the sin.

Hyssop (v. 7)—a small bushy plant that was used as a brush because of its small bunches of flowers. Hyssop was used to spread the blood of the lamb on the night of Passover (Exodus 12:22) and was also used in other cleansing rites by the priests.

Bloodguiltiness (v. 14)—guilt by the shedding of innocent blood (Deuteronomy 19:10). A person could incur bloodguilt in several ways, including murder, accidently causing someone's death, being responsible for a person who committed murder, or indirectly causing someone's death. In Matthew 27:24–25, Pilate refused to have bloodguilt because of Jesus' crucifixion, while the people in the crowd were willing to accept the responsibility.

Zion (v. 18)—the fortified hill southeast of Jerusalem which David conquered (2 Samuel 5:7). The term Zion was often used in the Old Testament to refer generally to Jerusalem.

> *Storm the throne of grace and persevere therein, and mercy will come down.*   JOHN WESLEY

THE WISDOM OF SOLOMON

Red Line Verse: *But if any of you lacks wisdom, let him ask of God, who gives to all generously and without reproach, and it will be given to him.* (James 1:5)

Red Line Statement: When God's people humbled themselves and sought God's help, God was always faithful to bless them with guidance and help them fulfill their calling.

Red Line Connection: God's people will always need God's help to live for Him, and God is willing to offer us the guidance we need to be successful in bringing glory to His name.

Focal Passage: 1 Kings 3

 Listen Attentively to the Lesson

1. Tell the story of 1 Kings 3:1–15 in your own words.

    Context: Eventually King Saul died and David became king over God's chosen people. David reigned over Israel for 40 years (1 Kings:2:11). Before his death, David proclaimed that his son Solomon was successor to his throne (1:28–40). David challenged Solomon to walk in his footsteps and be a God-honoring king: "I am going the way of all the earth. Be strong, therefore, and show yourself a man. Keep the charge of the LORD your God, to walk in His ways, to keep His statutes, His commandments, His ordinances, and His testimonies, according to what is written in the

Law of Moses, that you may succeed in all that you do and wher-
ever you turn, so that the LORD may carry out His promise which
He spoke concerning me, saying, 'If your sons are careful of their
way, to walk before Me in truth with all their heart and with
all their soul, you shall not lack a man on the throne of Israel.'"
(2:2–4).

Solomon would have many opportunities to choose God's
ways during his reign. Solomon and David had differing interests
and ideas about leading a nation, thus, their reigns would be
somewhat different. However, Solomon and David would have
some things in common. Both were men with human flaws, and
both men loved God, although the way their lives showed it
varied greatly.

2. Ask the small-group members to reconstruct the story of 1 Kings
   3:1–15 together, including as many details as they can remember.

3. Read the passage aloud together from Scripture, confirming the
   facts of the story. Amend any details suggested by small-group
   members that did not accurately represent the Scripture.

Investigate the Facts of the Lesson
Use these questions to guide small-group members to
investigate the facts of this passage.

1. Solomon was not perfect in following the ways of God. What
   errors in judgment does Solomon make in this passage (vv. 1–4)?

God wasn't pleased that Solomon offered sacrifices and burnt incense at the high places. Solomon also made a treaty with Egypt's king by marrying his daughter, two actions that were forbidden in Deuteronomy 7:1–3. (Solomon also would go on to have multiple wives, which was forbidden, and the warning of Deuteronomy 7:4 was realized for Solomon.) We can give Solomon credit for not allowing his Egyptian wife to dwell near the Ark of the Covenant (2 Chronicles 8:11).

2. Why were the people sacrificing at the high places (vv. 1–2)?

God chose Solomon to build the Temple (2 Samuel 7:12–13). Until the Temple was completed the Israelites were to continue worshipping at the Tabernacle. God had instructed that the high places of idol worship be destroyed (Numbers 33:52; Deuteronomy 12:2).

3. What was Solomon's relationship with God at this time?

Possible answer: Solomon loved and worshipped God, and he walked in His statutes. Solomon knew God, so much so that they openly communicated together. God's offer in 1 Kings 3:5 indicates God's desire to bless Solomon.

4. God gave Solomon the opportunity to ask for anything, and Solomon's answer revealed much about Solomon's heart.

a. What were Solomon's thoughts about himself (vv. 6–7)?

Solomon compared himself to his father David, a great king who prospered because of his faithfulness to God. Solomon knew that his role as king was critical, and he felt unprepared to be a great leader. Solomon called himself "your servant" in answering God.

b. What were Solomon's thoughts about God's people (vv. 8)?

Solomon had great respect for the fact that God had chosen Israel.

c. Based on Solomon's request, what was Solomon's focus?

Solomon's request doesn't indicate a focus on personal gain for himself, but instead he seemed focused on being an effective, wise leader for God's people. He wanted to be successful in completing the calling God had given him.

5. What other details do you see in this passage?

Allow your small group to share other details that stand out to them and discuss the significance of each point.

 Find the purpose of the lesson

Use these questions to guide small-group members to discover God's purpose for the passage.

1. In order to be a wise counselor, Solomon first had to receive wise counsel. Whom do you turn to for wisdom? Who is the first person you approach when you have a problem?

While Solomon had first received godly counsel from his father David, Solomon was now fully turning to God as His source of wisdom. Encourage your group to consider their preferred source of wisdom — is it God's Word, or wisdom from godly counselors, or the wisdom of the world?

2. Proverbs 12:15 teaches, "The way of a fool is right in his own eyes, but a wise man is he who listens to counsel." Rather than trusting in his own abilities, Solomon knew he needed God's counsel. What method do you use in your own life to determine if you're being "right in your own eyes"? Are you stubborn about insisting that your way is right, or are you quick to listen?

Be ready to share from your own life. Ask the group what Proverbs 12:15 says to them about any particular situation they are currently facing. Reference James 1:19.

3. (Small-group leader, summarize 1 Kings 3:16–28). Consider the reaction of Israel when they realized the wisdom of Solomon to administer justice (v. 28). Do you feel drawn to people who are filled with godly wisdom, or do you keep them at arm's length? Why?

   We often respect people who exhibit godly wisdom, but not everyone is willing to embrace wise people as close friends. Ask everyone to consider how they have chosen friends in various stages of life. As everyone shares, encourage your small-group members to surround themselves with people who will be wise traveling companions on the road of life.

4. Does God continue to grant wisdom to people who ask? Read James 1:5–8. What are the keys to asking for wisdom? What is "double-minded" about asking for wisdom without faith?

   God is still granting wisdom to those who ask for it. When we want wisdom, we must seek it from the proper source—God. We can ask boldly; He gives wisdom freely and without reproach. We must ask in faith, believing that God will answer our prayers. Otherwise, if we ask God for wisdom and then doubt that He will answer—or doubt that His answers to us are indeed the best course of action—we are being double-minded in our thinking.

5. What other truths from this passage stand out to you? What else can we learn about God or learn about being a follower of Christ?

   Allow everyone to respond. Share any other points of spiritual growth that the Holy Spirit brings to your attention.

Experience the Truth of the Lesson

Use these questions to guide small-group members to allow God's transformational truths to reshape their hearts and minds.

1. When you make requests of God in prayer, what do you typically ask God to do for you? Does your prayer life reflect a belief that God is able to do great things through you?

   Allow everyone to respond. Challenge your small group to evaluate how much of their prayer time is spent praying for the sick, praying for the lost, seeking God's direction, asking God for help, etc. Suggestion: if your small group typically shares prayer requests that only cover the sick and perhaps more non-personal needs, ask the group how they feel about taking the group's prayer times to a deeper level in the future, interceding for one another and seeking God's wisdom and guidance.

2. When was the last time you attempted to do something for God that you couldn't do in your own wisdom and strength? What are you currently longing for God to do in your life?

   Patiently pray as each small-group member thinks and then shares his or her answers.

3. How does Solomon's story relate to other men and women—including you—who have been recipients of redemption along God's thin red line?

   Solomon was a sinner, and yet he loved God and wanted to honor God in his life's calling as king. We all desperately need God's guidance in order to walk worthy of His calling.

4. Solomon so valued the wisdom God had given him above the other gifts (wealth, honor, and long life) that he wrote the Book

of Proverbs, a gift of God's wisdom. He strongly emphasized to the reader, "Get wisdom." What have you received from God that you would strongly encourage others to seek?

Lead in a discussion about the great gift of salvation and other gifts from God.

Between the Lines: Truth Points

City of David (v. 1)—Jerusalem is sometimes referred to as the City of David in the Old Testament (2 Samuel 5:6–10).

High places (v. 2)—Hebrew word meaning "elevation;" the high places were generally located on hills or places of natural elevation, where shrines were built for pagan worship.

Gibeon (v. 4)—means "hill place;" in the territory given to the tribe of Benjamin (Joshua 18:25). Gibeon was a city of significance in the days of David.

No matter how many books you read, no matter how many schools you attend, you're never really wise until you start making wise choices.
MARIE T. FREEMAN

Israel's Disobedience (Northern Kingdom)

Red Line Verse: *Thus I will afflict the descendants of David for this, but not always.* (1 Kings 11:39)

Red Line Statement: God split the territory of Israel into two kingdoms as a judgment against the idol worship of David's son Solomon, but God was faithful to maintain His plan for the Messiah to come through the descendants of David.

Red Line Connection: God remained consistent and patient. As His people were unfaithful, God remained faithful to keep His promises, knowing that His plan was unfolding and would eventually lead to the birth of our Messiah.

Focal Passage: 1 Kings 11:26–43

 Listen Attentively to the Lesson

1. Tell the story of 1 Kings 11:26–43 in your own words.

    Context: Solomon's reign was marked with much prosperity and wealth. God always keeps His word, and God had promised an understanding heart, riches, and honor to Solomon (1 Kings 3:12–13). However, Solomon did not always exercise the wisdom God had granted him. God appeared to Solomon a second time after he had finished building the Temple and his own palace, and God gave him a conditional promise: "As for you, if you will walk before Me as your father David walked, in integrity of heart and uprightness, doing according to all that I have commanded you and will keep My statutes and My ordinances, then I will establish the throne of your kingdom over Israel forever, just as I promised to your father David, saying 'You shall not lack a man on the throne of Israel'" (9:4–5).

Despite God's intimate conversations with Solomon and His plainly-spoken words, Solomon's heart turned toward other gods. Solomon took foreign wives, and his 700 wives and 300 concubines turned him away from God to worship false gods. Solomon the Temple builder was now building high places for false worship. God visited Solomon a third time to proclaim judgment upon him: "Because you have done this, and you have not kept My covenant and My statutes, which I have commanded you, I will surely tear the kingdom from you, and will give it to your servant. Nevertheless I will not do it in your days for the sake of your father David, but I will tear it out of the hand of your son. However, I will not tear away all the kingdom, but I will give one tribe to your son for the sake of My servant David and for the sake of Jerusalem which I have chosen" (11:11–13). Hadad the Edomite became Solomon's adversary, as well as Rezon in Damascus (11:14–25). However, the worst of the troubles for Solomon's kingdom was yet to come.

2. Ask the small-group members to reconstruct the story of 1 Kings 11:26–43 together, including as many details as they can remember.

3. Read the passage aloud together from Scripture, confirming the facts of the story. Amend any details suggested by small-group members that did not accurately represent the Scripture.

Investigate the Facts of the Lesson

Use these questions to guide small-group members to investigate the facts of this passage.

1. What prompted Jeroboam to rebel against the king (vv. 26–31)?

    Through the prophet Ahijah, God told Jeroboam He was giving ten tribes to him.

2. What kind of man was Jeroboam (v. 28, 40)?

    The young Jeroboam was a valiant warrior and also an industrious leader. When Jeroboam fled from Solomon, this was not necessarily a sign of weakness; David was a courageous warrior, but he also fled when Saul sought his life. However, it is worth noting that Jeroboam chose to flee to Egypt, which was a known location of God's enemies.

    79

3. We first hear of Ahijah and Jeroboam in this story. They didn't appear to be major players in the kingdom at the time of this meeting, and their conversation was held privately in a field (v. 29). However, the content of their conversation was a significant event in the history of God's people. What other times did God communicate big plans to largely unknown people in private settings? What is the significance?

    Possible answers: The angel privately announced to the young maiden Mary that she would give birth to the Messiah (Luke 1:26–38). Shepherds in the field were told of His arrival (Luke 2:8–14). God spoke to the shepherd Moses in the desert (Exodus 3). God does not need men in high places to execute His plans. God's will is going to be done because He reigns, not because the people He chooses to work through are well known, wealthy, or powerful.

4. What other details do you see in this passage?

    Allow your small group to share other details that stand out to them and discuss the significance of each point.

Find the purpose of the lesson

Use these questions to guide small-group members to discover God's purpose for the passage.

1. What did Solomon lose because of his disobedience?

    Possible answers: The kingdom wasn't split until after Solomon died. However, Solomon lost the opportunity to pass down a great legacy to his son, Rehoboam. Solomon wouldn't be able to have that peaceful, settled feeling on his deathbed, because he knew that his actions would bring troubles for his own son and for the entire kingdom. God had offered Solomon an established throne over God's people, and he discarded God's kindness because he lacked self-control. Solomon also lost the blessed opportunity to glorify God and point others to Him.

2. Solomon had the kingdom torn right from his hands. Have you ever had something taken from you? Did you feel entitled to it? Was Solomon entitled to the kingdom and the legacy?

    Sometimes we have a sense of entitlement because we feel we've worked hard to earn something, just as Solomon had put a great deal of effort into building the kingdom. However, Solomon was only on the throne to begin with because God placed him there, and God had the authority to remove him. Also, the kingdom only prospered financially because God allowed Solomon's kingdom to prosper. While it may appear that we've "earned" entitlements in life, God is the One who has all authority to give and take away.

3. God specifically mentioned three false gods: Ashtoreth, goddess

of love, fertility, and war; Chemosh (literally, *subdue*), the Moabites's god whom they believed would give them land, and Milcom, whose name means *king*. How are these particular gods a personal affront to God? Today, how are people tempted to look to other sources other than God for help on matters of love, family, the state of the nation, prosperity, and direction for their lives?

God had proven Himself faithful to the Israelites in all of these matters. How could Solomon turn to idols of wood and stone for guidance? How could Solomon worship idols when he had twice spoken directly to the living God? As you mention each issue the false gods were known for, allow your small group to discuss how the modern culture encourages us to look to science, economists, philosophers, politicians, physicians, etc., to give us what we need, giving no respect for the power and authority of God. How can we guard our hearts from falling into these worldly mindsets? How will we keep our hope firmly rooted in God alone?

4. Solomon's disobedience and lack of self-control resulted in the separation of God's chosen people, the recipients of God's promises He had initially made to Abraham.

   a. Compare God's promise to Jeroboam (1 Kings 11:37–38) to His promise to Solomon (9:4–5).

      God gave Jeroboam a similar conditional promise that began with the word "if."

   b. What measures did God take to keep His word to David and also maintain His "thin red line" plan of redemption (1 Kings 11:32, 34–36)?

      The Southern Kingdom, which would not be given to Jeroboam, would remain under the authority of the bloodline of David, and would include

Jerusalem. The Lion of Judah, Jesus Christ, was going to come from the bloodline of David. Note also that God said that His affliction against the descendants of David would not last forever (v. 39).

c. Consider all that Solomon was guilty of before God (v. 33). Is there any way to be successful in life when you aren't worshipping God or living by His standards?

We cannot expect to thrive when we aren't worshipping God in spirit and truth, and when we aren't living life by God's directives. Even when God places us in a position of spiritual authority (like Solomon on a throne), we will fail if we aren't worshipping God and living for Him. These simple truths can be easily overlooked if we take our focus off of Christ.

5. What other truths from this passage stand out to you? What else can we learn about God or learn about being a follower of Christ?

Allow everyone to respond. Share any other points of spiritual growth that the Holy Spirit brings to your attention.

Experience the Truth of the Lesson

Use these questions to guide small-group members to allow God's transformational truths to reshape their hearts and minds.

1. What are you planning to leave for your children (or the next generation)?

If wealth is what we desire to leave our children, we'll be motivated to amass more wealth and perhaps be self-controlled not to spend it all so we can leave something behind. If God's wisdom and family blessings are what we desire to leave with our children, we will be motivated to acquire more wisdom and hopefully be self-controlled to live under God's authority. Encourage everyone to discuss self-restraint and what lessons can be learned from what

Solomon's failure cost his son. More importantly, what had Solomon lost in the way of giving glory to God? How will we plan to leave a legacy of Christ's fame on the earth? How will we point people to place their faith in Jesus?

2. Solomon ultimately wasted God's promises. God then offered greatness to Jeroboam, but he also eventually turned from the Lord and became an evil schemer. God has promised you salvation through a relationship with Jesus Christ (Romans 10:9– 10). Wasting His promises or walking in them—what are you experiencing right now at this stage of your life?

   Allow your small group to share. Be prepared to share from your own life.

Between the Lines: Truth Points

Ephraimite (1 Kings 11:26)—the people group descending from Ephraim, one of the sons of Joseph, son of Jacob.

Millo (v. 27)— Hebrew word meaning filling; a fortress complex of walls at Jerusalem with earthen materials behind the exterior walls, providing strength and support.

Ten tribes for Jeroboam, one tribe for Rehoboam (vv. 31–32)—The twelve tribes of Israel originated from the twelve sons of Israel (Jacob). God gave specific instructions about how the territory of Israel was to be divided among them. The tribe of Levi was given no land allotment (Joshua 14:4). Two tribes sprang out of Joseph: Ephraim and Manasseh. When the Northern Kingdom (also called Israel, also called Ephraim) and the Southern Kingdom (also called Judah) split, the Southern Kingdom consisted of Judah and Benjamin, and all other territories were in the Northern Kingdom. (Simeon's territory was originally within the borders of Judah according to

Joshua 19:1, but true to Jacob's prophetic words in Genesis 49:5–7, they eventually became scattered throughout Israel.)

Rehoboam (v. 43)—the son of Solomon who was successor to Solomon's throne.

> *What do we Christians chiefly value in our leaders? The answer seems to be not their holiness, but their gifts and skills and resources. The thought that only holy people are likely to be spiritually useful does not loom large in our minds.* J.I. PACKER

THE REVOLT AGAINST REHOBOAM
(SOUTHERN KINGDOM)

● **Red Line Verse:** *"You must not go up and fight against your relatives the sons of Israel; return every man to his house, for this thing has come from Me."* (1 Kings 12:24)

● **Red Line Statement:** The Southern Kingdom, typically called Judah, remained under the authority of David's descendant; God commanded that His people not fight over the split.

● **Red Line Connection:** Jesus Christ is the One who will reunite all Jews as their King, and who unites all believers into one family, the family of God.

● **Focal Passage:** 1 Kings 12:1–24

 Listen Attentively to the Lesson

1. Tell the story of 1 Kings 12:1–24 in your own words.

Context: Solomon had learned of the prophet Ahijah's prophecy: Jeroboam would one day be given the ten northern tribes. Solomon was unsuccessful in his attempt to kill Jeroboam because Jeroboam fled to Egypt to avoid Solomon's sword (11:40). Solomon died and Rehoboam became king at age 41 (14:21). He reigned 17 years, walking in the ways of David and Solomon for his first three years, but forsaking God's law for the remainder of his reign (2 Chronicles 11:17; 12:1). Today's lesson focuses on how God's plan to divide the kingdom came to pass through Rehoboam's mistake early in his reign.

2. Ask the small-group members to reconstruct the story of 1 Kings 12:1–24 together, including as many details as they can remember.

3. Read the passage aloud together from Scripture, confirming the facts of the story. Amend any details suggested by small-group members that did not accurately represent the Scripture.

 Investigate the Facts of the Lesson

Use these questions to guide small-group members to investigate the facts of this passage.

1. How do we know that Jeroboam was considered a leader among the Israelites from the very beginning of Rehoboam's reign (I Kings 12:2–3)?

    The people sent for Jeroboam to return from Egypt when Solomon died. They remembered him from his days as their labor force leader, a position given to him by Solomon (11:28). In verse 20, we see the people calling for Jeroboam, and they chose him to be their king.

2. Why did the people assemble at Shechem (v. 1)? Why was Shechem potentially a good location?

    This assembly was an opportunity for the people to affirm their new king, following the pattern set when Saul became king (1 Samuel 10:17–27), and when David (2 Samuel 5:1–3) and Solomon (1 Kings 1:32–40) also entered their reigns. Shechem may have been chosen as an attempt to keep the tribes unified, since Shechem was a central location.

3. What was Rehoboam's first test as king? What did he do well, and what were his mistakes? What could have led Rehoboam to choose the advice of his friends? Perhaps your small group would give credit to Rehoboam for asking for three days to make a decision. He first asked for advice from the elders who had advised his father Solomon, and then he asked the friends he had spent time with since childhood. Note there is no evidence that Rehoboam consulted God.

Allow your small group to discuss Rehoboam's thought process in rejecting the advice of the elders and following his friends' advice. Why did he choose to be harsh toward the people? Sometimes pride causes a person to be a harsh leader, feeling that he or she is entitled to loyalty and respect because of a title or position. Insecurity can also be a cause of harsh behavior; people may feel that others will not freely respect them, so they try to command that respect with a show of force. Allow your small group to share from their personal experiences.

4. What other details do you see in this passage?

Allow your small group to share other details that stand out to them and discuss the significance of each point.

Find the purpose of the lesson

Use these questions to guide small-group members to discover God's purpose for the passage.

1. Rehoboam chose to be a heavy-handed leader and to speak harshly to his people.

   a. What was the leadership style that Jesus demonstrated to His followers?

Jesus taught us to be servant to all (Mark 9:35). Jesus set the example by washing His disciples' feet (John 13:4–11).

b. The elders advised that if Rehoboam would serve the people, the people would serve him as their king (1 Kings 12:7). Are you a willing servant of others? If you are in leadership over people, how do you serve that group of people?

   Allow your small group to respond. Reference Matthew 20:25–28.

2. What were the people expressing in verse 16? How could this attitude affect a church? What about a marriage? Did the people have an alternative choice to rebellion?

   Through Samuel, God warned the people they would pay a high price if they chose to have a king over them (1 Samuel 8:10–18). Israel learned the hard way that God was right. The people didn't feel any ownership in the kingdom, nor did they feel they were benefiting from the labors they had poured into it.

   Your discussion about God's Church and marriage may run parallel, since God's Word uses the imagery of God's people as the Bride of Christ. Remind everyone that when we serve the Lord through the church and also in a marriage, we are there to serve, not be served. We must examine our hearts when we become disgruntled in church or in a marriage because we "aren't getting out of it what we're putting into it." Discuss how a church or marriage suffers when those involved are only willing to serve when they feel they're benefiting from the relationship. In Israel's case, certainly Rehoboam was in the wrong, but so was Israel wrong. Flagrant rebellion against God's leaders is not God's way. Israel could have called upon God to intervene. They would suffer greatly because of this division, and Israel didn't bring glory to God before their enemies through this division.

3. When Rehoboam assembled warriors from his kingdom to fight against the northern kingdom, note the words of God in verse 24 as He stopped them from going to battle: "You must not go up and fight against your relatives the sons of Israel" (the NKJV reads, "your brethren the children of Israel").

   What is the message to people outside of God's family when the members within God's family fight against each other? What is Jesus' message in Matthew 12:25? In Matthew 12:25, Jesus taught that division brings ruination. Challenge everyone to take to heart the importance of peace within God's family as a witness to the world. Ask your group to consider how they will remember to apply this in their lives when they face a situation that they feel warrants a squabble within the family of God.

4. God told Rehoboam not to fight over or resist the division of the kingdom. God said, "This thing has come from Me" (v. 24).

   a. How had God allowed the free choices of everyone involved to bring about His will?

   Rehoboam and every party involved were completely responsible for their actions. God didn't cause anyone to sin and never will (James 1:13). However, God didn't intervene to stop Rehoboam; He had already made provision for this division by tapping Jeroboam to be the king of the northern kingdom. The division would bring hardship, and this hardship was punishment for idol worship in Israel.

   Take this opportunity to connect God's statement in 1 Kings 12:24 to God's sovereignty in the crucifixion of Jesus. In Peter's sermon on the Day of Pentecost, he called Jesus' death a "predetermined plan" under the "foreknowledge of God" (Acts 2:23), but Peter also clearly stated that the people were guilty for crucifying Jesus (Acts 2:36).

b. In your life, how do you know when to stop fighting against a terrible situation that is causing a broken relationship?

Allow your small group to share. Discuss the vital role of prayer for discernment. Discuss the hope we have in Christ, and that we are responsible to God in every relationship; we must continue to "fight the good fight" for reconciliation unless God confirms that the battle is over. Remind your small group that we are guilty before God if we are the cause of division in a relationship; Jesus said, "By this all men will know that you are My disciples, if you have love for one another"" (John 13:35).

5. What other truths from this passage stand out to you? What else can we learn about God or learn about being a follower of Christ?

Allow everyone to respond. Share any other points of spiritual growth that the Holy Spirit brings to your attention.

Experience the Truth of the Lesson

Use these questions to guide small-group members to allow God's transformational truths to reshape their hearts and minds.

1. Which person can you relate to most in this story: Rehoboam, the one who made a terrible mistake and then has to deal with the consequences? Jeroboam, the one who is able to step in to benefit from someone else's failures?

Or Adoram, the one who suffers while trying to be a peacemaker (1 Kings 12:18)? Allow your small group to share. Be prepared to share your personal connection.

2. God prophesied through Jeremiah that a day of reunification was coming (Jeremiah 3:18; 50:4). How does Jesus Christ bring unity? *Possible answers:*

- *Jesus is King of kings and Lord of Lords. One day, all will confess that He is Lord.*
- *Through Christ, the kingdoms of Judah and Israel are unified under one banner, one King.*
- *Now both Jew and Gentile are privileged to be brothers and sisters in the family of God.*
- *The veil in the Temple was torn in two when Jesus died on the Cross, and our relationship with God is restored through Jesus Christ.*
- *Jesus gives us the courage and wisdom to be agents of peace and restoration.*
    Encourage the group to make a personal connection to the unity Christ offers to them.

Between the Lines: Truth Points

Rehoboam (v. 1) — son of Solomon and grandson of David, who was king over the Southern Kingdom, also known as Judah, after the kingdom split. David was from the tribe of Judah.

Shechem (v. 1) — city in the tribal land of Ephraim, 40 miles north of Jerusalem. Shechem became the first capital of the Northern Kingdom (12:25).

Jeroboam (v. 2) — the Ephraimite whom God had selected to be the first king over the Northern Kingdom, Israel (11:26–38). Jeroboam is perhaps best known for leading the Northern Kingdom to participate in idol worship by setting up shrines and high places, having idols crafted, establishing a new feast schedule, and appointing priests who were not of the tribe of Levi (12:25–33).

Ahijah (v. 15) — the prophet of God who told Jeroboam he would be king over the Northern Kingdom (11:29–38).

Adoram (v. 18)—abbreviated version of the name of Adoniram.

Judah and Benjamin (v. 21)—the two southern tribes that comprised the Southern Kingdom, also known as Judah.

Shemaiah (v. 22)—prophet of God to Rehoboam (see also 2 Chronicles 12:5–8).

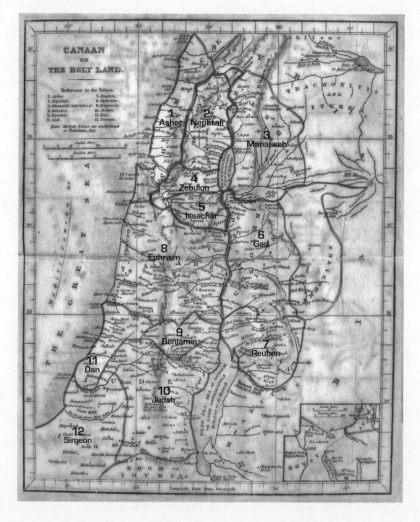

Nations, like individuals, are subjected to punishments and chastisements in this world. ABRAHAM LINCOLN

CONQUERED AND WAITING

When the nation of Israel crumbled, it appeared that this once great people were utterly defeated. Where was God? And what of His promises? While it appeared that God's enemies were now in control of the world order, little did they know that God was still holding all things in place, maneuvering the "thin red line" closer to the arrival of the promised Savior. Even when God's people are rebellious and unfaithful, the Almighty is always faithful and true.

In the dark hours of human history when Israel lay in utter ruination, God was all the while preparing to shine a brilliant light over the little town of Bethlehem. In our era it may also appear that God's enemies have staged a mutiny and are now holding the reins of this world where evil is celebrated, but take cheer. Because of the promise of redemption, we know that He is in control even now, preparing to shine the light of Jesus Christ into the darkest corners of the world.

LIFE LESSON 24

GOD PUNISHES AND PROTECTS: DANIEL

Red Line Verses: *He is the living God and enduring forever, and His kingdom is one which will not be destroyed, and His dominion will be forever. He delivers and rescues and performs signs and wonders in heaven and on earth.* (Daniel 6:26–27)

Red Line Statement: Both Judah and Israel were eventually conquered by their enemies. During this time of defeat and occupation, God provided godly leaders and prophets who proclaimed His Word and witnessed of the one true God before both Jew and Gentile. God performed signs and wonders to testify of His glory.

Red Line Connection: God uses His servants to display His glory among the peoples of the earth.

Focal Passage: Daniel 6:1–28

 Listen Attentively to the Lesson

1. Tell the story of Daniel 6:1–28 in your own words.

   Context: After the children of Israel split into two kingdoms, both kingdoms suffered from inconsistent leadership, and more importantly, inconsistency in their relationship with God. Because of their disobedience and idol worship, both kingdoms eventually fell to conquering nations of the pagan world. Israel, the Northern Kingdom, fell in the eighth century B.C. to the Assyrians, while Judah, the Southern Kingdom, held on until early sixth century B.C., when they were conquered by the Babylonians. It was during this time that Daniel and other Hebrew young men of Judah were taken to King Nebuchadnezzar's palace to be trained as skilled servants for the Babylonians (1:1–6). When Babylon was later conquered by the Persians, Daniel continued to serve reigning kings with integrity, remaining faithful to God above all.

2. Ask the small-group members to reconstruct the story of Daniel 6:1–28 together, including as many details as they can remember.

3. Read the passage aloud together from Scripture, confirming the facts of the story. Amend any details suggested by small-group members that did not accurately represent the Scripture.

Investigate the Facts of the Lesson

Use these questions to guide small-group members to investigate the facts of this passage.

1. Consider what we learn about the character of Daniel in Daniel 6:1–4.

   a. What kind of man was he?

   As a captive from Judah, Daniel was an outsider (v. 13), yet he had proven to be a faithful leader, standing out above the rest. King Darius thought very highly of Daniel, and Daniel's jealous counterparts could find no fault in his work ethic or loyalties to the king. They also knew Daniel was a fervent follower of God, indicating he was open with his faith.

   b. Is a spirit of excellence a unique gift from the Lord; is it based on environment, or is every Spirit-filled Christian able to have a spirit of excellence?

   Allow your small group to respond.

2. When Daniel learned the decree was signed, he went home (v. 10).

   a. What did Daniel do at home?

   Daniel talked to the One who had ultimate authority over his life—he talked with God.

b. What were the contents of Daniel's prayers?

We don't know all that Daniel prayed, but we do know that he gave thanks.

3. What explanation did Daniel give for why he was saved from the lions (v. 22)? What reason does verse 23 give for Daniel's deliverance? How does Acts 5:29 relate?

Daniel said God saved him because he was innocent before God; verse 23 indicates Daniel was spared because "he trusted in his God." Though we are to obey those in authority over us (Titus 3:1), Acts 5:29 teaches that God's law trumps man's law.

4. What is the significance of what happened to Daniel's accusers (v. 24)?

Possible answers: God brought justice by allowing the false accusers to be killed the way they had planned for Daniel to die. The lions' vicious attack showed that they were hungry wild animals; it had to be a supernatural event that the lions didn't kill Daniel.

5. What other details do you see in this passage?

Allow your small group to share other details that stand out to them and discuss the significance of each point.

Find the purpose of the lesson

Use these questions to guide small-group members to discover God's purpose for the passage.

1. When Daniel was brought to Babylon as a captive in his youth, he experienced the first test of his faith when he was offered the king's delicacies (1:5). Daniel passed the test and "made up his mind that he would not defile himself" (1:8).

a. What was the defining moment in your life when you purposed in your heart not to defile yourself with the world's pleasures?

Allow everyone to share, and be prepared to share your story.

b. God gave Daniel opportunities through the years to increase in wisdom, to grow strong in the Lord, and to build his faith in God. He prepared Daniel for this great personal challenge. What wisdom, strength, and faith have you gained through undergoing trials?

Allow everyone to share their stories.

c. Daniel went home and prayed "as was his custom since early days" (Daniel 6:10 NKJV). How did his consistent prayer life affect his ability to endure this challenge of his faith?

Prayer is communication with God, and we draw strength from Him. Daniel doesn't appear to be praying in desperation, nor was Daniel praying simply in angry defiance of the decree. Ask your small group — do some people pray only in desperate times? Do some people pray or act openly religious only in defiance — in those times when they're told their religious rights are being taken away? How does our consistency in prayer honor God?

2. The satraps, governors, and King Darius thought Daniel would surely suffer a horrible death because the decree couldn't be reversed according to the law of the Medes and Persians. Daniel's enemies rejoiced and Darius mourned, thinking that Daniel's fate was certain. Think about the Cross. Jesus breathed His last, and God's enemies rejoiced while Christ's followers mourned. The scene was bleak, but God's resurrection power triumphed in the end. What is God saying to you about His authority over the events of your life? Over the events of this world?

As Christ's return draws near, circumstances for Christians as well as for all people will grow bleaker just as God's Word has foretold. However, we can carry ourselves with a quiet confidence in God, just as Daniel did. "'In quietness and trust is your strength'" (Isaiah 30:15). Even in our daily trials, we must remember that unbelievers are watching us and learning what we believe about God by our response to situations that seem hopeless.

3. This story is as much about what God taught Darius as it is about what He taught Daniel.

    a. What kind of relationship did Daniel have with King Darius? What kind of relationship do you have with the lost people in your life?

    Darius had a great respect for Daniel as a man of excellence, and he trusted Daniel. Darius had a deep affection for Daniel as well. He was angry with himself for signing a decree that would cause Daniel to be put in the lions' den, and he tried to undo the matter. Darius did not sleep the night Daniel was in the den. Ask your small group to share about their daily interactions with the lost. Are they living above reproach as a witness? Are they extending kindness and friendship to the lost?

    b. Before Daniel ever entered the lions' den, what had Darius already learned about God by observing the life of Daniel (v. 16)? What does Darius's early morning behavior at the den reveal about what was going on in his heart (vv. 19–20)?

    Note in verse 16, Darius said "your God." He knew that Daniel served God continually, but he specified that this was the God of Daniel, not of Darius. In verse 16 we also see a glimmer of faith, that perhaps Darius knew that this God of Daniel's was a deliverer. In verse 19, Darius went early in the morning, and he went personally; the king didn't send a servant to learn of Daniel's fate. Did Darius have hope that Daniel was alive? Perhaps, because he called out to Daniel, hoping for a response. Note that Darius referred to God as the living God, and the wording speaks to his heart's question: was God capable of saving Daniel?

   c. According to Darius's decree in verses 26–27, what had Darius come to believe about the living God?

     Spend time thoroughly examining these verses, praising God for each truth.

4. What other truths from this passage stand out to you? What else can we learn about God or learn about being a follower of Christ?

    Allow everyone to respond. Share any other points of spiritual growth that the Holy Spirit brings to your attention.

Experience the Truth of the Lesson

Use these questions to guide small-group members to allow God's transformational truths to reshape their hearts and minds.

1. Darius learned of the faithfulness, power, and authority of God in a very real way because he was an eyewitness of God at work through Daniel's persecution. Are you exercising spiritual disciplines today to prepare to be used by God in the future? Are you open to God using you to bring others to Him?

    As everyone shares, challenge your small group to consider seriously what God wants to do in their lives to bring others to Christ, even if it means suffering. Share 1 Peter 4:13.

2. God delivered Daniel, and He still delivers today. However, God doesn't always spare Christians from persecution, and Christian persecution around the world is increasing. What does the

suffering of believers have to do with the *thin red line?*

God's plan of redemption extends to all nations, including those nations persecuting Christians. God can use the patient suffering and unrelenting faith of Christians as a witness to the world. These verses offer wisdom for how we as Christians should respond to persecution: Matthew 5:10–12, 5:44; Romans 12:14; Hebrews 13:3.

Between the Lines: Truth Points

Darius (Daniel 6:1)— King of Persia. Daniel was first brought into this region of the world as a captive of the Babylonians, who were later conquered by the Persians under the leadership of Cyrus.

Satrap (v. 2)—Persian political leader who governed a territory called a satrapy.

Law of the Medes and Persians (v. 8)—the Persian kingdom overtook the Median kingdom around 550 B.C., but the Medes continued to have a place of honor in the Persian Empire. The region of Media was so important to the Persian Empire that Persian kings were called the kings of Media and Persia (8:20).

Signet (v. 17)—a seal, often crafted on a ring, that carried the weight of a person in authority. The signet's seal, pressed in hot wax, was much like a signature.

> *If the price of which you shall have a true experience is that of sorrow, buy the truth at that price.*   C.H. SPURGEON

LIFE LESSON 25

LETTING GOD USE US AS GOOD EXAMPLES

Red Line Verse: *"The God of heaven will give us success; therefore we His servants will arise and build."* (Nehemiah 2:20)

Red Line Statement: God moved the hearts of foreign kings to allow the Jews who were under captivity to reunite and rebuild Jerusalem, God's chosen city.

Red Line Connection: God works among the remnant to bring restoration.

Background Passages: Ezra 1:1–7; Nehemiah 1–10

Focal Passage: Nehemiah 4

 Listen Attentively to the Lesson

1. Tell the story of Nehemiah 4 in your own words.

   Context: In 586 BC, the Babylonians destroyed Jerusalem's walls, gates, and temple (2 Kings 25:1–21). The Persians later conquered the Babylonians, placing the captive Jews under Persian rule. About 50 years after Jerusalem's fall, God moved the heart of the Persian King Cyrus to make a decree: "'The LORD, the God of heaven, has given me all the kingdoms of the earth and He has appointed me to build Him a house in Jerusalem, which is in Judah. Whoever there is among you of all His people, may his God be with him! Let him go up to Jerusalem which is in Judah and rebuild the house of the LORD, the God of Israel; He is the God who is in Jerusalem. Every survivor, at whatever place he may live, let the men of that place support him with silver and gold, with goods and cattle, together with a freewill offering for the house of God which is in Jerusalem'" (Ezra 1:2–4).

Cyrus also returned all that had been stolen from the Temple when Nebuchadnezzar conquered Jerusalem (Ezra 1:7). About 42,000 Jews returned to Jerusalem, worship was restored, and temple restoration began (Ezra 2:64–3:13).

The Jews soon faced outside resistance; the Persian king that followed Cyrus halted temple building. When King Darius came to power, he researched the matter, and honored the original decree of Cyrus (Ezra 4:1–6:12).

About 70 years after the Temple was rebuilt, Nehemiah learned that Jerusalem's gates and walls were still in disrepair, and that the remnant of Jews now residing in Jerusalem were in distress. Nehemiah was an important official as the cupbearer for the Persian King Artaxerxes, and the king granted Nehemiah a commission to return to Jerusalem to rebuild the wall. Nehemiah was a man of prayer who not only had the blessing of his king, but the blessing of the Lord. When Nehemiah arrived, he shared his vision with the leaders of Jerusalem, and the work began. However, Nehemiah would face much opposition in his endeavor to lead the rebuilding of the walls of Jerusalem (Nehemiah 1–3).

2. Ask the small-group members to reconstruct the story of Nehemiah 4 together, including as many details as they can remember.

3. Read the passage aloud together from Scripture, confirming the facts of the story. Amend any details suggested by small-group members that did not accurately represent the Scripture.

Investigate the Facts of the Lesson

Use these questions to guide small-group members to investigate the facts of this passage.

1. What was at the heart of the ridicule from Sanballat and Tobiah (Nehemiah 4:1–3)? What were they saying about the Jews' endeavor to rebuild the walls, and what were they trying to accomplish? Together, examine the sarcasm of Sanballat and Tobiah.

    They wanted to break the spirit of the people. They wanted the Jews to feel weak, defeated, discouraged, and humiliated.

2. As Nehemiah and the Jews made progress, the neighboring people groups banded together to plot against the Jews' attempt to grow strong again (vv. 7–8, 11). When Nehemiah positioned the people, what did he say to encourage them (v. 14)? What did Nehemiah want them to focus on?

    Instead of focusing on the enemy, Nehemiah encouraged the Jews to remember their God and to fight for their families and their people.

3. Once Nehemiah and the Jews realized they had enemies who were willing to kill them to stop their progress, how did they restructure their assignments in order to stay on guard (vv. 16–23)? How is the rebuilding of the wall a great picture of cooperation among God's people?

    Half the servants did construction while girded with a sword, and the other half stood by fully armed, with the leaders behind them. They developed a system of communication, using a trumpet to sound a warning. Nehemiah also asked the people to stay overnight in Jerusalem for further protection. Each family or group worked together to build a portion of the wall, with each person doing his part (Nehemiah 3). The people were unified in purpose and they rallied behind their leader, even during times of adversity.

4. What other details do you see in this passage?

Allow your small group to share other details that stand out to them and discuss the significance of each point.

Find the purpose of the lesson
Use these questions to guide small-group members to discover God's purpose for the passage.

1. Nehemiah responded to the attacks against them with prayer, and his prayers were filled with words of righteous indignation (vv. 4–5, 9). How can we as Christians do battle on our knees against the enemies of God and still fulfill Christ's command in Luke 6:27–29?

As your small group shares, encourage everyone to think about the love of Christ for even His enemies. We can pray that evildoers will not be successful in their charge against Christianity while also praying for their salvation. Ask your small group if they are praying for people who are currently attacking Christianity, and how God is prompting them to pray. Challenge everyone to take seriously the call of Christ to pray for our enemies.

2. Think about how the Jews became watchful and prepared to defend themselves.

a. Did their awareness of the threats slow down their work? Should we as a church slow down our missions and ministry when we sense the enemy threatening?

They didn't allow the threats to become a distraction. While the obvious answer to the second question is "no," encourage a thoughtful response from everyone.

b. The Jews became watchful. What does watchfulness look like in your personal walk with Christ? What does watchfulness look like for a church?

Allow everyone to respond. Encourage your small group to realize that we face different temptations and trials, but the same enemy. Reference 1 Peter 5:8.

c. The armor of God is our weaponry, given to us by God for our spiritual battles against the enemy (Ephesians 6:11–17). Read Ephesians 6:13. God wants us to be able to stand firm against our enemies. How do you see the Jews standing firm against their enemies in this story?

The Jews had work to do. They were in Jerusalem to build a wall and strengthen the city. They didn't desire to fight, but they were prepared to defend themselves if necessary. They stood up to their enemies by carrying on the work despite their threats. Encourage everyone to think about what standing firm looks like in their own lives.

3. The Jews were fighting for their brethren and for their families (v. 14).

a. What are the enemies of today's families?

Possible answers: drug and alcohol abuse, acceptance of casual sexual activity and abhorrent sexual lifestyles, universalism, greed, the elevation of leisure activities and hobbies to idol status, busy-ness, the breakdown of family units.

b. What pressures are you currently facing from society that threaten your family?

Encourage a specific and personal response.

c. Nehemiah was the Jews' leader, and his response to the threats had a direct impact on the safety of each family and also the rebuilding of the wall. You are a leader in your home. Your response to the threats against your family's spiritual health will have a profound impact on your family's walk with God and your family's success in fulfilling your calling in God's kingdom. Do you feel like you have a choice in your family's lifestyle? Do you feel that you are leading your family or that circumstances and schedules lead you? What choices are you making to defend your family?

As your small-group members respond, encourage them to realize they have the right to make choices for their family that may go against society's norms. Connect the firm stand of Nehemiah as leader to your small-group members' choices as the leaders in their homes. Nehemiah's people had to make sacrifices, and we as Christians must also be willing to make sacrifices if it means fulfilling our calling and defending the spiritual health of our families.

4. According to verse 10, what other discouragements did the Jews face? Can you relate?

   The workers were growing weary, and it took extra effort for them to clear away the rubbish in order to build the wall. Discuss how "rubbish" wearies us as we seek to do God's work.

5. What other truths from this passage stand out to you? What else can we learn about God or learn about being a follower of Christ?

   Allow everyone to respond. Share any other points of spiritual growth that the Holy Spirit brings to your attention.

Experience the Truth of the Lesson

Use these questions to guide small-group members to allow God's transformational truths to reshape their hearts and minds.

1. Progress on the wall was swift, because "the people had a mind to work" (v. 6). As you think back over your life, when have you most had a mind to work for the Lord?

   Be prepared for a pause while your small-group members think through their responses. Encourage everyone to respond personally as much as they feel comfortable.

2. God allowed the Hebrew people to be scattered because of their disobedience, and during Nehemiah's day God reunited them and gave them the honor of rebuilding Jerusalem. The Jews responded by rekindling their passion and understanding of God's Law, by repenting of their sin, and by making a covenant with God (Nehemiah 8–10). Read Nehemiah 9:1–3. The people recounted their history with God and concluded, "You are just in all that has come upon us; for You have dealt faithfully, but we have acted wickedly" (9:33).

   a. Why is this event significant in the history of God's chosen people?

      This event displays God's grace and His gift of restoration. God will once again reunite the children of Israel (Ezekiel 20:34; Isaiah 11:11–12).

   b. How is this story a model for revival today?

      The Jews spent hours in worship and study of God's Word, and the reading of God's Word led to their confession of sin. God restored them as a people, and He will do the same today.

   ## Between the Lines: Truth Points

Sanballat (Neh. 4:1) — According to records from the reign of Darius I, he was governor of Samaria. Sanballat's daughter was married to the grandson of Jerusalem's high priest (13:28). It appears likely that Sanballat's opposition to the rebuilding of Jerusalem was about maintaining wealth and power in that region. Sanballat was a Horonite (13:28).

Tobiah the Ammonite (v. 3)—Scholars indicate that Tobiah was a practicing Jew who resided in the Temple area.

Arabs (v. 7)—Arab was a city in Judah near Hebron.

Ammonites (v. 7)—descendants of Lot through his incestuous relationship with his younger daughter; she bore a son named Ben-ammi (Genesis 19:36–38)

Ashdodites (v. 7)—Ashdod was a principle city of the Philistines. It was allocated to the tribe of Judah as a piece of the Promised Land (Joshua 15:46–47). Uzziah actually captured this city and placed it under Israel's control (2 Chronicles 26:8), but the city didn't remain under Israel's control for long.

> *To know that God rules over all—that there are no accidents in life, that no tactic of Satan or man can ever thwart the will of God—brings divine comfort.* KAY ARTHUR

LIFE LESSON 26

Prophecies of Jesus

Red Line Verse: *For a child will be born to us, a son will be given to us; and the government will rest on His shoulders; and His name will be called Wonderful Counselor, Mighty God, Eternal Father, Prince of Peace.* (Isaiah 9:6)

Red Line Statement: The prophets foretold of the coming Messiah who would fulfill God's covenant promises and His divine plan for the redemption of mankind.

Red Line Connection: Jesus fulfilled all of the prophecies of the Messiah.

Background Passages: Isaiah 53; Jeremiah 23:5–6; Micah 5:2; Acts 3:13–14, 25–26

Focal Passage: Isaiah 9:1–7

 Listen Attentively to the Lesson

1. Tell the message of Isaiah 9:1–7 in your own words.

   Context: Throughout the early history of the Jews, God made covenants with Abraham and his descendants that pointed to the impending arrival of the Messiah. The prophetic books of the Old Testament also point to the arrival of a Savior with great clarity and with many specific details that pertain to the life, death, and resurrection of Jesus. This lesson is a wonderful opportunity to help small-group members reconnect with the thin red line of redemption from creation to the era of the prophets who foretold Jesus the Messiah.

2. Ask the small-group members to reconstruct the message of Isaiah 9:1–7 together, including as many details as they can remember.

3. Read the passage aloud together from Scripture, confirming the facts of the passage. Amend any details suggested by small-group members that did not accurately represent the Scripture.

Investigate the Facts of the Lesson

Use these questions to guide small-group members to investigate the facts of this passage.

1. Verse 1 begins with "but" (NASB) or "nevertheless" (NKJV), indicating that Isaiah is drawing a contrast between what he has been writing about and what he is about to foretell. Isaiah 8 foretold an Assyrian invasion and great distress for both Israel and Judah.

   a. What have you learned through the *Thin Red Line* about the pain and sorrows of the children of Israel since the days of Abraham? What was the cause of their sorrows?

   Guide your small group to review the times of bondage, famine, wandering, defeat, plunder, humiliation, false worship, internal strife and other sorrows the Jews faced because of sin.

b. How does mention of Galilee (the land of Zebulun and the land of Naphtali) in verse 1 point us to Jesus?

Jesus fulfilled this prophecy, as Matthew pointed out in Matthew 4:12–16.

2. Isaiah prophesied that Messiah would sit on David's throne (v. 7). Look back to God's promise to David in 2 Samuel 7:16. How does Jesus connect to David? How is it possible for Jesus the Messiah to reign forever?

David's name is listed in Matthew 1:6 as an ancestor of Jesus. Jesus is God's Son and eternal; He is the great I AM, who was and is and always will be, and His authority and power assures us that He can and will reign forever.

3. God especially noted in verse Isaiah 9:7 that this prophecy would come to pass.

a. Who was going to be responsible for fulfilling this prophecy (v. 7)?

God was going to make this happen, according to His great zeal. Note to your small group that it would be virtually impossible for any person to fulfill the many prophecies concerning the Messiah of his own determination; only God could provide our Savior, and only Jesus fulfills the prophecies.

b. What are some of the events we've studied along the *thin red line* thus far that show how zealous and determined God was to redeem His people?

Allow your small group to share. Possible answers (from "Thin Red Line" series, volumes one and two): preserving mankind through Noah; the Israelites's escape from Egyptian bondage; the guidance of the judges God provided even while the Israelites went after foreign gods.

4. What other details do you see in this passage? Allow your small group to share other details that stand out to them and discuss the significance of each point.

Find the purpose of the lesson

Use these questions to guide small-group members to discover God's purpose for the passage.

1. Examine the spiritual blessings God promised in verse 2.

a. What happens when a person tries to walk in darkness? What is it like to live in total spiritual darkness?

Possible answers: a feeling of being lost with no direction; fear; danger; no peace; feelings of isolation; no hope. Encourage your small group to realize that this is what their lives were like before they met Christ, and this is the way of life for those who are still without Christ.

b. Imagine a land covered in shadows, like a shroud of death hovering over society every moment of every day. Are there places on the earth where spiritual and physical death hovers over the people all the time? For those who have always lived in such darkness, surrounded by the presence of death, what would it be like for them to experience that light for the first time?

Allow your small group to respond. Discuss the amazing joy that would flood over a city if they experienced the beauty and warmth of light for the first time. This is a picture of how God transforms a person, a family, a village, or even a nation when they are introduced to Jesus Christ, the Light of the World. Ask your members to consider: would you like to be used by God to bring light to a people who live in darkness?

c. How does God's promise in Isaiah 49:6 connect you to the *thin red line* of redemption?

> *God was not satisfied to send His Son to be the Light of the World for the Jews only. God gave Jesus to be a light to the Gentiles as well so that every nation could experience salvation.*

2. Isaiah 9:3–5 prophesied about the quality of life for those who received Jesus the Messiah.

   a. What are the blessings that Jesus Christ gives us? What are the sorrows that He takes away?

   > *He gives us joy, like those who are celebrating harvest or who are dividing the spoils of victory. He gives us freedom by removing the yoke of burden, the staff, and the rod of an oppressor. He gives us peace by ending fighting and bloodshed.*

   b. Which one of Christ's blessings are you experiencing in abundance today? Which one are you struggling to possess at this time in your life? Why?

   > *Encourage each person in your small group to respond. To help them, you may want to give the following as possible choices: joy like celebrating a harvest or victory, freedom from burden or oppression, or peace from the end of fighting and bloodshed.*

3. Isaiah's description of the Messiah in verse 6 is a beautiful description of Jesus. What are some stories from the New Testament that show Jesus fulfilling these descriptions? How has Jesus fulfilled these roles in your life as your personal Savior?

   > *Encourage your small group to have both New Testament stories as well as personal stories. Possible New Testament stories:*

- *A Child*—Jesus was born as a baby (Luke 2:1–7); note that this truth also makes Jesus the fulfillment of God's promise to Adam and Eve (Genesis 3:15).
- *A Son*—Jesus let Nicodemus know that He was the Son of God (John 3:16).
- *Dominion*— Jesus told Pilate that His kingdom was not of this world (John 18:36). His authority is above every earthly kingdom.
- *Wonderful*—Jesus raised Lazarus (John 11:38–44).
- *Counselor*—Jesus was a counselor to Mary and Martha (Luke 10:38–42).
- *Mighty God*—Jesus walked on water and controlled the wind (Matthew 14:22–33).
- *Everlasting Father*— This descriptor of Jesus should not be confused with the distinction of three persons in the Trinity. Jesus is the Son of God the Father. As Everlasting Father, Jesus is the source of, or "father of," all that is everlasting and eternal. The resurrection of Jesus gives us a confident hope that we also will live forever with Him (Luke 24:1–8).
- *Prince of Peace*—Jesus brought peace to the demoniac (Mark 5:1–20).

4. Not all of Isaiah's prophecies about Jesus are filled with pleasant words. God also told Isaiah to prophesy of the sufferings of Christ. Read Isaiah 53 together. What words or phrases from this prophecy stand out to you? Why? How do Jesus' attributes and actions described in Isaiah 53 support and fulfill how Jesus is described in Isaiah 9:1–7?

   Allow everyone to share freely. Encourage your small group to remember that Christ had to suffer and die in order to bring us the gifts described in Isaiah 9:1–7. Also, Jesus' life described in Isaiah 53 is no less powerful and mighty than how we see Him in Isaiah 9:1–7.

5. What other truths from this passage stand out to you? What else can we learn about God or learn about being a follower of Christ?

Allow everyone to respond. Share any other points of spiritual growth that the Holy Spirit brings to your attention.

Experience the Truth of the Lesson
Use these questions to guide small-group members to allow God's transformational truths to reshape their hearts and minds.

1. How will you serve in Christ's kingdom to help others experience all of who Jesus is?

   Allow your small group to respond. Encourage them to think of people who need to know the Savior. Discuss how Isaiah 9:1–7 helps us better understand the many ways we are blessed through Jesus, and how the lost need to experience the fullness of His identity. We all need to know Jesus as Counselor, as the Eternal One, as Prince of Peace, etc.

2. You have now spent several weeks examining the Old Testament foreshadowing of Jesus and the unfolding of God's plan of redemption. How has this look into the Old Testament prepared your heart to begin studying the New Testament with new perspective?

   Be prepared to share what God has shown you over the many weeks of enjoying this study.

Between the Lines: Truth Points

Zebulun and Naphtali (v. 1) — land allotments that were part of the Northern Kingdom of Israel, originally given to two of the sons of Jacob; this area suffered defeat and plunder from the Assyrians. This area came to be known as Galilee of the Gentiles when it came under Gentile domination. Jesus also ministered in this area.

The day of Midian (v. 4)—God delivered the Israelites by defeating Midian in the days of Gideon (Judges 7:1–24).

Wonderful (v. 6) — exceptional, distinguished.

Everlasting Father (v. 6)—Jesus is a member of the Trinity, and thus He is one with the Father. However, this idiom is perhaps best understood in how Jesus relates to time, and not in how He relates to God the Father. Jesus is eternal, and we will live forever through Him.

> *The hope we have in Jesus is the anchor for the soul — something sure and steadfast, preventing drifting or giving way, lowered to the depth of God's love.* FRANKLIN GRAHAM

WEEKLY PREPARATION FOR SMALL-GROUP MEMBERS

Would your small-group members like to prepare for each week's lesson? Consider these two options.

OPTION 1: A Private Walk with God

When we learn to open God's Word and let the Holy Spirit be our Teacher, God can pierce our hearts with the specific truths that are relevant to our daily needs. With the "A Private Walk with God" option, each small-group member is invited to take a private walk with God through the Scripture, friend to friend, for one-on-one time alone with God. Imagine how each person will grow, draw near to God, and deepen their love for the Word when they hear the words of God falling personally upon their own ear. One Teacher, one student.

Provide the "A Private Walk with God" tool for each small-group member, encouraging them to keep the tool tucked in their Bible for easy reference. Each week, provide the focal passage for the upcoming lesson to your small group, and ask small-group members to read through the passage using these questions, recording their reflections in a notebook or journal. In your weekly small-group discussions, commend the efforts of those who are contributing to the discussion based on how God has spoken to them through their "A Private Walk with God" weekly preparation.

THIN RED LINE

Preparing for the Lesson: A Private Walk with God

Find a quiet place to sit alone with your Bible, a notebook or journal, and the following set of questions. Each week, read through the focal passage several times, and ask God to be your personal Teacher, and you His student. Pray for personal insights and life application as well as biblical knowledge. Enjoy this time alone with God! Every child of God can hear His voice speaking to us directly from the Scriptures; we need only to listen. Whether in a thundering voice or a gentle whisper, He will speak to you.

> *As for you, the anointing which you received from Him abides in you, and you have no need for anyone to teach you; but as His anointing teaches you about all things, and is true and is not a lie, and just as it has taught you, you abide in Him.*
>
> — 1 JOHN 2:27

1. What are the key words that stand out to you in this passage?

2. What is the main idea of this passage? Is there more than one theme?

3. What does this passage reveal about who God is?

4. What does this passage reveal about what it means to be a disciple of Christ?

5. Is there a truth or a phrase from this passage that is particularly meaningful to you in your current life circumstances? How can this truth or phrase strengthen your walk with Christ?

6. Is there a word, phrase, or verse that you have questions about? If so, write down your questions. Pray and ask the Holy Spirit to increase your understanding. Read the passage again.

7. Ask God to help you apply the truths of this passage today. If this time of study has brought to mind any prayer requests you can bring to God about your friends, family, church, nation, or world, talk with God about these prayer concerns.

OPTION 2: Awaken Your Mind

Provide a copy of the printable "Awaken Your Mind" small-group member preparation guide. You may choose to incorporate these additional questions into your weekly small-group time, or another option is to encourage your small group to engage in online discussions of these questions in preparation for your small-group gathering.

OBEDIENCE MATTERS: THE FALL OF JERICHO

● ──── **Red Line Verse:** *There are things under the ban in your midst, O Israel; You cannot stand before your enemies until you have removed the things under the ban from your midst.* (Joshua 7:13)

● ──── **Red Line Statement:** God continued faithfully to keep His covenant, but the people struggled with sin, resulting in devastating consequences.

● ──── **Red Line Connection:** Sin has terrible consequences and blocks the flow of God's blessings.

● ──── **Focal Passage:** Joshua 6–7

Questions to Consider:

1. Why were the children of Israel defeated in battle (Joshua 7:12)?

2. What did God require of the children of Israel before they could go forward in victory (v. 13)?

3. What method did God use to reveal the culprit (vv. 14)?

4. How was the wrath of God satisfied (vv. 25–26)?

GOD BEARS WITH HIS PEOPLE: THE JUDGES

Red Line Verse: *Yet they did not listen to their judges, for they played the harlot after other gods and bowed themselves down to them. They turned aside quickly from the way in which their fathers had walked in obeying the commandments of the LORD; they did not do as their fathers.* (Judges 2:17)

Red Line Statement: God's people broke their covenant with God by committing idolatry and intermingling with wicked nations, yet God was still merciful to send godly leaders to help His people overcome their enemies.

Red Line Connection: Mankind is unfaithful, yet God is faithful. Even though we don't deserve His love and protection, God is patient with His people and redemption is His great gift.

Focal Passage: Judges 2:7–19

Questions to Consider:

1. Where did the Hebrews learn about the false gods they started to worship (Judges 2:12)?

2. How did God show mercy to the Hebrews, despite their rebellion (vv. 16, 18)?

3. How was the idolatrous behavior of the Hebrews like "playing the harlot" (v. 17)?

4. What could bring a people to reject the God who had brought deliverance to their forefathers and instead choose to bow down to idols?

GOD BLESSES THE FAITHFUL: RUTH

Red Line Verses: *He saved us, not on the basis of deeds which we have done in righteousness, but according to His mercy, by the washing of regeneration and renewing by the Holy Spirit, whom He poured out upon us richly through Jesus Christ our Savior.* (Titus 3:5–6)

Red Line Statement: While God had chosen the children of Israel as His own special people, God also redeemed others who turned to Him in faith.

Red Line Connection: Ruth is a picture of God's grace and redemption. She was born an enemy of God, but she turned to God and He embraced her, redeeming her and offering her a new life.

Focal Passage: Ruth 1

Questions to Consider:

1. When Naomi began her journey back to Bethlehem, what did she instruct her daughters-in-law to do (Ruth 1:8–15)?

2. What are the specific pledges that Ruth made to Naomi (vv. 16–17)?

3. What was the state of Naomi's heart when she returned to Bethlehem (vv. 20–21)?

4. How is Ruth a model of faithfulness?

Challenge: Read the entire Book of Ruth. How was God's timing perfect, bringing Naomi and Ruth back to Bethlehem at the beginning of barley harvest (v. 22)?

A YOUNG AND FAITHFUL SERVANT: SAMUEL HEARS FROM GOD

Red Line Verse: *Samuel grew and the LORD was with him and let none of his words fail.* (1 Samuel 3:19)

Red Line Statement: God provided prophets and priests to lead and guide His people into righteousness.

Red Line Connection: The prophets God appointed provided great spiritual leadership to the Israelites and their leaders. They offered guidance and also pointed the Israelites to look toward their future King of kings.

Focal Passage: 1 Samuel 3

Questions to Consider:

1. There was a lack of prophecy and revelation from God during this era (1 Samuel 3:1). Why would this feel like a punishment to the people?

2. Why didn't Samuel recognize God's voice (v. 7)? How do you recognize the voice of God (John 10:4–5)?

3. What was the price Eli would pay for putting his relationship with his sons before his relationship with God (v. 13)?

4. How did God establish Samuel in his ministry (vv. 19–20)?

MISUSE OF GOD'S BLESSING: THE DEMISE OF KING SAUL

Red Line Verse: *Much more then, being now justified by his blood, we shall be saved from wrath through him.* (Romans 5:9 NKJV)

Red Line Statement: God provided a means for the people to receive forgiveness of their sins through the sacrificial system, and God required that His plan be followed exactly.

Red Line Connection: God has provided redemption for mankind through Jesus Christ, and God requires that all people go through Jesus Christ and Him alone for forgiveness of sin.

Focal Passage: 1 Samuel 13:1–14

Questions to Consider:

1. What kind of pressure was Saul under while waiting in Gilgal (vv. 5–8)? How was Saul being tested?

2. How long did Saul wait before offered the burnt offering (v. 8)? How much time elapsed between Saul's burnt offering and the arrival of Samuel (v. 10)?

3. Why did Saul feel compelled to offer a burnt offering and peace offering before going into battle against the Philistines (v. 12)?

4. What was so "foolish" (v. 13) about Saul's actions?

GOD'S POWER ON DISPLAY:
THE BOY AND THE GIANT

Red Line Verse: *The LORD does not deliver by sword or by spear; for the battle is the LORD'S.* (1 Samuel 17:47)

Red Line Statement: God raised up for the Israelite people a great king named David who demonstrated that salvation comes in the name of the Lord.

Red Line Connection: David was important in the bloodline of Messiah. Jesus was often called "Son of David" (Matthew 21:15). Just as David called upon the name of the Lord and was saved, God has promised salvation to all who call upon His name (Acts 2:21).

Focal Passage: 1 Samuel 17

Questions to Consider:

1. When David talked with the men of Saul's army about Goliath, what was their focus (1 Samuel 17:25)?

2. When Eliab personally attacked David's character, how did David respond (v. 29)? How do you respond when you are personally attacked by a loved one or by a member of the family of God?

3. What was David's expectation as he entered into combat against Goliath (v. 46–47)?

4. Try to imagine this event from Saul's perspective. What did God teach him through this experience? What did God teach Eliab? The Israelite army? The Philistines?

REPENTANCE AND RESTORATION: DAVID

Red Line Verses: *Be gracious to me, O God, according to Your lovingkindness; according to the greatness of Your compassion blot out my transgressions. Wash me thoroughly from my iniquity and cleanse me from my sin.* (Psalm 51:1–2)

Red Line Statement: The sin of God's people brought shame and sorrows upon them, but God's forgiveness of those who repented brought restoration, renewal, and rejoicing.

Red Line Connection: God has consistently displayed a willingness to forgive repentant sinners.

126

Background Passage: 2 Samuel 11–12:24

Focal Passage: Psalm 51

Questions to Consider:

1. How does God use "broken bones" to restore us (Psalm 51:8)?

2. In Psalm 51:5, David traced his sinful nature back to the very beginning of his conception. What is David referring to?

3. What did David say to express his desire to joyfully bring praise to God?

4. David knew God wanted him to have a broken and contrite heart. When have you experienced brokenness in your life?

The Wisdom of Solomon

Red Line Verse: *But if any of you lacks wisdom, let him ask of God, who gives to all generously and without reproach, and it will be given to him.* (James 1:5)

Red Line Statement: When God's people humbled themselves and sought God's help, God was always faithful to bless them with guidance and help them fulfill their calling.

Red Line Connection: God's people will always need God's help to live for Him, and God is willing to offer us the guidance we need to be successful in bringing glory to His name.

Focal Passage: 1 Kings 3

127

Questions to Consider:

1. What kind of relationship did Solomon have with the Lord (v. 3)? How does it compare with your relationship with the Lord?

2. In light of Solomon's request of God, what was weighing upon Solomon's heart (vv. 6–9)? What was Solomon's focus as the king over God's people?

3. Note what God remarked that Solomon did not ask of God (v. 11). Why do you think God mentioned these specific requests that Solomon did not make?

4. What are some of the key words in God's conditional promise to Solomon in verse 14?

ISRAEL'S DISOBEDIENCE (NORTHERN KINGDOM)

Red Line Verse: *Thus I will afflict the descendants of David for this, but not always.* (1 Kings 11:39)

Red Line Statement: God split the territory of Israel into two kingdoms as a judgment against the idol worship of David's son Solomon, but God was faithful to maintain His plan for the Messiah to come through the descendants of David.

Red Line Connection: God remained consistent and patient. As His people were unfaithful, God remained faithful to keep His promises, knowing that His plan was unfolding and would eventually lead to the birth of our Messiah.

Focal Passage: 1 Kings 11:26–43

Questions to Consider:

1. Solomon had been given great wisdom from God, yet he made such terrible choices. How is it possible to have God's wisdom and still make sinful choices?

2. Read verse 33. When we don't do what is right in God's eyes, to whom are we looking to tell us what is right and wrong? Do you see this happening in the world today?

3. God promised that David's descendants wouldn't be afflicted over this kingdom separation forever (v. 39). Why is this promise of God important? Who will reunite all tribes of Jews, and also unite all the peoples of the earth?

4. Solomon tried to kill Jeroboam when he learned of God's declaration (v. 40). How did this show a lack of understanding from Solomon?

THE REVOLT AGAINST REHOBOAM
(SOUTHERN KINGDOM)

Red Line Verse: *"You must not go up and fight against your relatives the sons of Israel; return every man to his house, for this thing has come from Me."* (1 Kings 12:24)

Red Line Statement: The Southern Kingdom, typically called Judah, remained under the authority of David's descendant; God commanded that His people not fight over the split.

Red Line Connection: Jesus Christ is the One who will reunite all Jews as their King, and who unites all believers into one family, the family of God.

Focal Passage: 1 Kings 12:1–24

Questions to Consider:

1. Try to identify with Rehoboam as he faced his first challenge as king and failed. What was at the heart of his poor response to the people?

2. When the people revolted against Rehoboam, what was their reasoning (v. 16)?

3. God said of the division, "This thing is from Me" (v. 24). How does God's division of the kingdom ring true with what He had said from the beginning in His promises to the children of Israel?

4. As you think about the many characters in this passage, who would you identify as guilty parties in this story? Who is innocent in this story?

GOD PUNISHES AND PROTECTS: DANIEL

Red Line Verses: *He is the living God and enduring forever, and His kingdom is one which will not be destroyed, and His dominion will be forever. He delivers and rescues and performs signs and wonders in heaven and on earth.* (Daniel 6:26–27)

Red Line Statement: Both Judah and Israel were eventually conquered by their enemies. During this time of defeat and occupation, God provided godly leaders and prophets who proclaimed God's Word and witnessed of the one true God before both Jew and Gentile. God performed signs and wonders to testify of His glory.

Red Line Connection: God uses His servants to display His glory among the peoples of the earth.

Focal Passage: Daniel 6:1–28

Questions to Consider:

1. What distinguished Daniel from the other governmental leaders (vv. 3–5)?

2. What character flaw do you see in Darius that led him to fall into the plot of his officials (vv. 6–9)?

3. What kind of relationship did Daniel have with King Darius?

4. Consider Darius's decree in Daniel 6:26–27. What did God do to prompt a pagan king like Darius to declare the matchless power and authority of God? What is God doing today to display His glory among the nations?

LETTING GOD USE US AS GOOD EXAMPLES

Red Line Verse: *"The God of heaven will give us success; therefore we His servants will arise and build."* (Nehemiah 2:20)

Red Line Statement: God moved the hearts of foreign kings to allow the Jews who were under captivity to reunite and rebuild Jerusalem, God's chosen city.

Red Line Connection: God works among the remnant to bring restoration.

Background Passages: Ezra 1:1–7; Nehemiah 1–10

Focal Passage: Nehemiah 4

Questions to Consider:

1. What were the obstacles that Nehemiah and the people faced as they rebuilt the wall?

2. What evidence do you see that Nehemiah saw the rebuilding of the wall as an act of service to the Lord (Nehemiah 4:4–5, 9, 14–15, 20)?

3. As the construction workers built with a tool in one hand and a weapon in the other (v. 17), how is this a picture of the Christian life?

4. What motivated the people to stand firm against their enemies as they built the wall (v. 14)?

Prophecies of Jesus

Red Line Verse: *For a child will be born to us, a son will be given to us; and the government will rest on His shoulders; and His name will be called Wonderful Counselor, Mighty God, Eternal Father, Prince of Peace.* (Isaiah 9:6)

Red Line Statement: The prophets foretold of the coming Messiah who would fulfill God's covenant promises and His divine plan for the redemption of mankind.

Red Line Connection: Jesus fulfilled all of the prophecies of the Messiah.

Background Passages: Isaiah 53; Jeremiah 23:5–6; Micah 5:2; Acts 3:13–14, 25–26

Focal Passage: Isaiah 9:1–7

Questions to Consider:

1. What words or phrases in this passage describe Jesus as bringing joy, freedom, and peace?

2. As a Christian who knows Jesus personally, how have you found the words of Isaiah 9:1–7 to be true of your personal Savior?

3. Which of the descriptors of Jesus in verse 6 means the most to you personally?

4. Try to imagine hearing this prophecy as a Jew living in the days of the prophets, suffering and scattered from the effects of sin. How would this prophecy bring you hope?

SAMPLE LESSON FROM VOLUME 3 IN THE "THIN RED LINE" SERIES

LIFE LESSON 36

FINAL MOMENTS BEFORE THE ARREST

Red Line Verse: *"For this is My blood of the covenant, which is poured out for many for forgiveness of sins."* (Matthew 26:28)

Red Line Statement: Jesus ate the Passover with His disciples and instituted communion as a remembrance of Christ's life given as a new covenant between God and mankind.

Red Line Connection: Jesus was the sacrificial Lamb of God whose body was broken and blood shed to give us a new covenant with God.

Focal Passages: Matthew 26:20–30, 36–42

 Listen Attentively to the Lesson

1. Tell the story of Matthew 26:20–30, 36–42 in your own words.

    Context: After Jesus' triumphal entry on Sunday, He cleansed the Temple, taught, prophesied, and healed the sick while the battle raged among the religious leaders over Jesus' identity. The chief priests and scribes were plotting to kill Him, but feared the people (Luke 22:2). Judas Iscariot, one of Jesus' twelve disciples, approached them and agreed to betray Jesus for 30 pieces of silver (Matthew 26:14–16). On Thursday evening, Jesus ate the Passover as His last meal with His disciples (26:17–19). It was the night before His crucifixion, and Jesus would teach His disciples many lessons in these final hours.

2. Reconstruct Matthew 26:20–30, 36–42 together, including as many details as your small group remembers.

3. Read the passage aloud together from Scripture, confirming the facts of the story. Amend any details suggested by small-group members that did not accurately represent the Scripture.

Investigate the Facts of the Lesson

Use these questions to guide small-group members to investigate the facts of this passage.

1. The week had already been potentially stressful for the disciples. Sunday's triumphal entry created a stir throughout Jerusalem, and the Pharisees and scribes were outraged.

   a. What was the terrible news Jesus gave the disciples during the Passover meal (v. 21)?

      One of the disciples would betray Jesus.

   b. What was the response of the disciples (v. 22)? What do their responses reveal about what may have been going on in their hearts?

      They were deeply sorrowed, and each man asked Jesus if he were the guilty one. Ask your small group to explore why the disciples would ask such a question. Were they feeling weak? Were they struggling under the pressure from the Pharisees? Were they afraid? Did each man feel he was capable of being the betrayer?

c. Were the disciples showing spiritual maturity or immaturity by asking Jesus, "Surely not I, Lord?"

Allow your small group to respond. We can at least appreciate the disciples' great sorrow over this news that someone would betray Jesus; brokenness over sin is a mark of spiritual maturity. We can also admire their willingness to be honest and transparent with Jesus as each of them asked Jesus if he was the guilty one.

2. This last meal with the disciples was significant because they were celebrating Passover.

a. When God instituted the celebration of the Passover in the days of Moses, what was the reason for the annual celebration (Exodus 12:27)? What were the Jews supposed to remember?

God wanted the Jews to remember for all generations that the death angel passed over them when the firstborn of Egypt were struck during the tenth and final plague that led to the deliverance of Israel out of Egyptian bondage. They were saved from death by the blood of a sacrificial lamb.

b. What did Jesus tell His disciples was the reason for them to partake of the bread and wine (vv. 26–28)? What did Jesus want them to remember?

Jesus wanted them to remember His broken body and shed blood. Jesus said, "Do this in remembrance of Me" (Luke 22:19).

3. In the garden, what was the "cup" Jesus prayed about (v. 39, 42)? What was Jesus' ultimate desire that He expressed in His prayer?

What does Jesus teach us about prayer?

Above all, Jesus wanted to do the will of the Father, and He taught us to pray for God's will to be done above our own desires. Your small group may have many ideas to express the meaning of the "cup" Jesus spoke of in His prayer to the Father, because Jesus was about to suffer many things. However, emphasize the magnitude of Jesus taking the sins of the world upon Himself (2 Corinthians 5:21; 1 Peter 2:24). He experienced the full effects of sin, including the feeling of separation from the Father (Mark 15:34). The cup of God's wrath was poured out upon Jesus.

4. What other details do you see in this passage?

Allow your small group to share other details that stand out to them and discuss the significance of each point.

Find the purpose of the lesson

Use these questions to guide small-group members to discover God's purpose for the passage.

1. What was the value for Judas to know that Jesus was aware of his betrayal? How are you personally challenged by knowing that Jesus knew Judas was the betrayer, and yet He washed Judas's feet (John 13:1–5), didn't respond to Judas in anger, and didn't try to stop Judas?

Jesus submitted to His Father's will and displayed amazing self-control that challenges us to reconsider how we should respond to people who hurt us. Would the Lord also allow us to endure hardships with difficult people so that God can achieve a greater purpose in our lives or in their lives? Are we willing to serve others who aren't showing kindness to us?

2. Jesus spoke of His blood shed for a new covenant (v. 28). Read Hebrews 8:8–13. Why did God offer a new covenant? How is grace extended in the new covenant? What words and phrases in Hebrews 8:8–13 speak to the intimate relationship that God offers us in the new covenant?

> *The Israelites didn't keep the covenant God had made with their fathers (v. 9). The new covenant is a great display of God's grace, as God promises to remember our sin no more. Our unrighteousness is met with His mercy.*

3. Blood sacrifices had always been an integral part of God's requirements for the pardon of sin: "without shedding of blood, there is no remission of sins" (Hebrews 9:22 NKJV).

137

a. How did Jesus' sacrificial death on the Cross replace the need for animal sacrifices?

> *Jesus was without sin, the only perfect sacrifice as the Lamb of God. His blood alone is able to atone for the sins of all of mankind and purchase our salvation. Refer to 1 Peter 3:18.*

b. Because the Jewish Christians of the early church had experienced blood sacrifices, the taking of the Lord's Supper was surely a strong visual for them to remember Jesus' sacrifice on the Cross. As someone who has never had to experience blood sacrifices, how do you personally relate to the image of the bread and wine when you partake of the Lord's Supper?

> *Encourage your small group to discuss the significance of the Lord's Supper and ask them if they will approach the Lord's Supper any differently after studying how the Lord's Supper conveys God's message of the thin red line of redemption.*

4. In the garden, Jesus told Peter, James, and John about His deep sorrow, and He asked them to "keep watch" with Him (v. 38). Instead, they fell asleep.

a. How does it affect you when you know people are praying with you about a matter?

Ask everyone to think about the prayer support they offer one another as a small group.

b. The disciples let Jesus down by falling asleep in His time of sorrow. If they had realized what was about to happen, do you think they would have taken the prayer time more seriously? What keeps us from taking prayer more seriously?

Be prepared to share how prayer has made a difference in your life. Guide an open discussion about how our prayer lives can be strengthened by realizing how vital our communication with God is.

5. What other truths from this passage stand out to you? What else can we learn about God or learn about being a follower of Christ? Allow everyone to respond. Share any other points of spiritual growth that the Holy Spirit brings to your attention.

Experience the Truth of the Lesson

Use these questions to guide small-group members to allow God's transformational truths to reshape their hearts and minds.

1. When Jesus instituted what we now call the Lord's Supper, He told the disciples to partake of the bread and wine; He wanted them to personally experience it by taking in the food and drink.

As a Christian, how are you personally connected with Jesus' death on the Cross?

Guide your small-group members to fully embrace the sacrifice that Jesus made on the Cross to pay the penalty for their sins. Jesus redeemed us; His blood purchased our salvation. Ask them how their lives have been changed by believing that Jesus didn't choose to die just for some abstract concept of "sin in the world," but He chose to give His life on the Cross so that He might purchase our salvation.

2. The disciples didn't know what was about to happen in the garden, but Jesus did. He told Peter to "keep watching and praying that you may not enter into temptation; the spirit is willing, but the flesh is weak" (v. 41). You also don't know your future, but God does. Read verse 41 again, allowing Jesus to give these instructions to you for today. How can a person live practically by the words of verse 41?

   Challenge everyone to embrace Christ's words for a lifestyle of prayer and watchfulness.

3. Which scene from this study has gripped your attention more today — the scene around the table for the Passover meal or the events in the garden of Gethsemane? Why?

   Encourage every person to share an answer.

Between the Lines: Truth Points

"Surely not I, Lord?" (v. 22) — The wording of the question in the negative suggests that each disciple expected to hear "no," yet each man asked the question rather than emphatically denying that he could be the betrayer. (Later in the evening, Peter denied that he could ever stumble in his loyalty to Jesus when Jesus made the statement in verse 31, "You will all fall away because of Me this night.") Also note that the disciples' reaction to Jesus' news that there was a betrayer among them seemed to be shock; Judas had hidden his evil intents well.

Hymn (v. 30) — Particular Psalms were designated to be recited as part of the Passover celebration in homes as well as in the Temple as Passover lambs were being slain. These groupings of Psalms were called "Hallel" or "Praise Thou." Scholars believe that Psalms 113 to 118 were recited in homes, thus one of these passages may have been the hymn that Jesus and the disciples sang before going to the Mount of Olives.

Gethsemane (v. 36) — means "oil press." Located on the Mount of Olives.

Two sons of Zebedee (v. 37) — James and John.

Joy in affliction is rooted in the hope of resurrection, but our experience of suffering also deepens the root of that hope.

JOHN PIPER

FOR MORE

"THIN RED LINE" SERIES RESOURCES, GO TO:

http://www.newhopedigital.com/ThinRedLine

WorldCrafts^{SM} develops sustainable,
fair-trade businesses among impoverished people
around the world.

The WorldCrafts Support Freedom campaign
actively empowers WorldCrafts buyers and
aids artisans by highlighting those groups involved
in human trafficking and sexual exploitation.

Learn more about the campaign, purchase products
in the campaign, download our prayer guide,
and learn how to mobilize others by going to
WorldCrafts.org/SupportFreedom.asp.

WORLDCRAFTS^{SM}

Committed. Holistic. Fair Trade.

WorldCrafts.org 1-800-968-7301

WorldCrafts is a division of WMU®.

Bible Study On the Go!

Interact. Engage. Grow.

New Hope Interactive is a new digital Bible study platform that allows you to unlock content to download your favorite New Hope Bible study workbooks on your tablet or mobile device. Your answers and notes are kept private through a profile that's easy to create and FREE!

Perfect for individual or small group use!

To learn more visit NewHopeInteractive.com/getstarted